MW00902404

MODERN
LOVE

"Awakening the chambers of the human Heart"

LUKE
HOLTER

Preface

Endorsements

"My granddaughter was in the backseat of a car having a conversation but there was no one else in the backseat. When her mom asked who she was speaking with, my granddaughter respectfully responded, "Jesus." When her mom asked what the Lord said to her my granddaughter replied, "that I was created for love." She was five at the time. What a profound revelation entrusted to a young and pure heart. The message of love is clearly one that will be emphatically embraced and demonstrated in these last days. Luke Holter has captured this reality in his new book, "Modern Love" and awakened us to our Father's desire to manifest Love in His people. The principles in this book will clearly help each reader press in to this biblical heritage and secret for the harvest."

Paul Keith Davis
White Dove Ministries

"I am in Luke Holter's cheering section as he releases "Modern Love" in this critical hour of reformation. It will empower you through grace and truth to raise the bar of your faith, values, and your walk in Christ. I highly recommend this book for both personal reading and to use as a study tool in groups."

Patricia King
Founder, XPmedia

Special Dedication
This book is dedicated to my wife Grace Holter...

Grace, you came into my life at a time when I needed your namesake the most. You have been a constant blessing to me as a husband, friend, and man of God. I would not be the man I am today without your backbone and quiet strength. Some men stand alone in their greatness, but I stand with you in our greatness and in the Lord's strength. Being married to you has brought so much beauty into my life. You are a powerful, prophetic, and wise woman of God. I am so blessed to have you in my life and along with me on this journey.

You remind me to be the man I am called to be and for that I thank you...

Acknowledgements: A special thank you to God, Jesus, and the Holy Spirit (it is for you that I wrote this book, I pray it pleases you) Grace Holter, Barry & Cheri Holter, Mike & Joy Myers, the Laurel Family, the DE Castro Family, Grandma & Grandpa Holter, Grammi & Grampi DE Castro, Grandma & Grandpa Laurel, The Holmes Family, the Salazar Family, Heidi Kratzke, Andrew Heard & Christian Tabernacle, Mark & Jeannie Holter, Darin Crawford (now you're a man), Patricia King, Shawn Bolz, Paul Keith Davis, Paul Cain, Dave & Tina Wagner, LaVonne Chandler, Kathy Hahn, The Elijahlist, the Caldwell Family, Randy Caldwell Ministries, Calvin Campbell, the Thomas family, Drew & Christi Becker, Freedom Worship Center, Kurt & Lisa Chaffee, New Song Church, and, of course, Mike Bickle for his wisdom and teachings (I am thankful for the years you poured into me at IHOP).

Preface

"How do you fall in love with an idea?" "How do find a love that is stronger than any love you have ever felt on this earth?" These questions haunt me. I feel at times that I am a big fan of God, but do not feel as if I am in love with Him. I know that the love we feel for our families and spouses is different, but even in that our love for God should be different and greater than the love of family or spouses. How do we get our hearts to match what we know in our minds?

From my own experience and education I have become personally charged to work with the Holy Spirit to align our hearts and vision. It is issues like love that can separate us from each other or bring as close as brothers. Jesus always loves well, without ever failing to radiate love in the most pure, gentle, powerful, and perfect way. My own questions about this type of love started me on a journey to discover true love. I am on a quest to witness the transforming power of seeing myself and others through the filter of the Holy Spirit.

As believers we have an awesome invitation to view situations in life through the filter of the Holy Spirit. We have an opportunity to embark on a journey of reconciliation. Both sinner and saint have this invitation of reconciliation from God. I believe that the primary motivation to reach the lost as well as the primary motivation for the lost to want salvation hinge on the power of God's love. It is out of this incomprehensible love that a plan was birthed in Heaven and a baby on this earth.

I have found myself on a journey of discovery as it relates to the modern church and love. I have been studying the scripture totally possessed by a mandate from God to understand love, become a vessel of love, and raise others to thunder love in this world. I believe that we are a generation that will love in a remarkable way. This generation is desperate to receive love and to be able to dispense that love to others.

In this book I will share many stories both inspiring and heart breaking. My own life rings true of desperation to be loved. My story is that of a lovesick, lost, and desperate person. I have chased after versions of love and found myself in moments of great weakness trying to connect to love. Through reading these stories, coupled with prophetic insight, I pray you will find the strength required for your own journey.

My hope is through this book you will gain a greater understanding of the power of the Holy Spirit to reconcile our vision and thoughts to the heart of the Father. I have gained a great reward by availing myself to the Holy Spirit for the purpose of transforming my vision. The great reward I am speaking of is the ability to view others with the filter of love. You as well can receive a great reward by setting yourself aside and asking the Holy Spirit, "Give me dove's eyes. Let me see myself and others as you do."

When deciding to write a book on the topic of

love and perspective, I found myself on a personal search for what qualifies me to write on such a powerful and broad topic. I am 33 years old and starting to look back into my life and personal history. It is not that I believe that I am at an age where my life story needs to be told. I am still quite a young man in more ways than I think I care to admit. My father and mother raised me in a Christian home and I am a second generation preacher. Most of what I learned of love was from the world and not the mother and fathers of the church.

I have done my best to love others at those specific times of my life when I chose to love. It is funny how you can look back at your life and remember when you thought you were making good decisions and you thought you loved others with only the best intentions and motives. This is where I am looking back at my history and being charged in my spirit to further delve into this topic of love. Now I don't mean to give the impression that I have no qualifications for writing on a topic like this. I have learned many things from my relationships with others as well as my time spent as a Christian counselor. In my education I have spent countless hours reading, researching, and living this message of love.

Chapter one

A Business Model for Love

Some of the most revealing things about your theology on the Godhead are what you believe about love, what you think of love, and the way you interact with the world around you. Many people say many things that they do not mean or truly believe as it relates to belief systems. Often times we get trapped in popular Christian statements and we regurgitate this information without ever really getting revelation and change from it. It has become all too easy to lump our character and nature into blanketing statements that we believe make us powerful or attractive to ourselves and others.

We must fight the urge to portray ourselves in a way that is not accurate. In the same breath we must view our surroundings and world with the same discerning eye. Having a fair, truthful, and accurate view of ourselves and the world around us does not mean that we are overly critical of ourselves and the world. It does not mean that we operate under false humility considering ourselves nothing. It means we find strength in the truth of who God is and who we are in God. It means that we let ourselves off the hook when necessary and we hold our feet to the fire when necessary.

I had a very close friend and I remember a story he

told me about a girl he was head over heels in love with. This young man was from the poor side of town and this young lady was from the part of town with all the money. He told me he met this young lady at a concert and they were totally smitten with one another. They dated for about a month and then she came to visit him on his side of town. When she saw that kind of family he came from as well as what she thought his future potential was, well then she decided that he was no longer the right fit for her. When she told my friend that she no longer wanted to see him, he asked her why? Her answer was it just doesn't make sense to be together we are from two different worlds and I need someone who will be successful fiscally. Now this is a pretty mild example of placing business value on others, and yet it's all too real to ignore.

As a culture we have replaced what we use as a compass relating to finding and recognizing love and value. Business is our new compass. I believe that as a generation we have been taught to replace love and value with business. I do not literally think that we look at love as a business, although that could be an arguable issue. I do, however, believe that the business world, rather than the heart, has brought about what we have determined as success relating to the issue of love.

When we talk about the view of the world we are not simply speaking of the geography. We are also talking about other people and how we interact with them under the filter of our upbringing and experiences. The problem with consumerism in modern

Christianity is that it teaches an entirely inhumane system of measuring human value. We look at others in our sphere of influence as a commodity rather than a unique individual who has needs. In part, this desensitizing has to do with the amount of sexuality we are bombarded with in the media. There is no denying that there is a large amount of unhealthy sexuality that is attached to consumerism. When you couple consumerism and inappropriate sexuality it dehumanizes us one to another. With sexuality and business we learn that our boundaries are not established in love but rather carnally minded value. This brings the issue of poor boundaries into the equation. When we use a business mindset then sexual encounter is the prize that we win, but when love is our compass the sexual encounter becomes something to honor and protect. Often when we have a business mindset we do not value something in the same way as when love is in the equation.

When we stop putting the right kind of value on others and ourselves it causes isolation in our hearts as well as in our actions towards others. Our culture is driven by the desire to become powerful and unaffected by our environment. We evaluate our need to be loved or love others based on what attributes are of value to us in the equation. We measure our value and the value of others based on attractiveness and financial wealth. The problem with this view of the world and ourselves is that it produces failure and disappointment. When we do not measure up to the value system of our day and age, it produces striving and insecurities that cripple our self-image and our image of the world around us.

In the 21st century, we look at attraction, love, and character in a much different light then that of our forefathers. Customs have changed and so has our culture. It is worth asking the question: What have we gained and what have we lost in the process of the forward motion of society? In early western society, it was a very detailed and lengthy process to get two individuals to come into a relationship and agree to marriage. Marriage and companionship were not something that people just flippantly fell into. Marriage and relationship took thought and counting the cost of that kind of relationship.

We learn from the work of psychologist Erich Fromm that people in modern society often look at the ability to love as a relatively simple thing. In actuality, most of the time we have no real intimate connection with the things we say we love. We are a generation that has been raised with estranged love and worth. Young people today are being raised to love objects rather than explore and learn about what loving really entails. We are raised with the idea that we must learn what it means to become lovable rather than the understanding that we already are loveable. Our attention and hope become fixated on finding someone to love or for someone to find us worth extending love to. People are confusing "romantic affection" with love. Please don't misunderstand me; I believe that love is present in many lives in the world. I am just seeing a fast crisis in the last two generations relating to what love is. I know that I myself fall into this category and that, in part, is the reason for this journey you are reading about.

There are several powerful writings from Psychologist Erich Fromm that will add a depth of understanding that time nor experience has allowed me as of yet. Erich Fromm was a psychologist from the early 1900's and at the end of his life He was associated with what became known as the Frankfurt School of critical theory. I actually read about Mr. Fromm in some of my textbooks on psychology. I later went to Barnes and Noble and purchased a wonderful book titled "The Art of Loving" and in this wonderful book Mr. Fromm writes: "This attitude-that nothing is easier than to love-has continued to be the prevalent idea about love in spite of the overwhelming evidence to the contrary. There is hardly any activity, any enterprise, which is started with such tremendous hopes and expectations, and yet, which fails so regularly, as love. If this were the case for any other activity, people would be eager to know the reason for the failure and to learn how one could do better – or they would give up the activity. Since the latter is impossible in the case of love, there seems to be only one adequate way to overcome the failure of love – to examine the reasons for this failure and to proceed to study the meaning of love.

We as human beings must understand that love was never meant to be something quite as damaging and clumsy as we have made it. Love is a powerful thing that could change the entire planet for the better, if we only knew how to harness this power in truth and wisdom. Love is not just something we do but it is something we posses and can give out to others. It is a very tangible tool we have.

To think of love as a tool may help you get to the process of learning about love. Just think about love in an analogy of a painter and a paintbrush. If you are going to paint a picture you must know as much as you can about the tools you are using. You would not just walk into an art supply store and spend over two thousand dollars on art supplies that you know nothing about. Love in this respect is an art and you must learn the theory and you must practice to master that art."

When perceiving love through the business model, it is easy to lose sight of love as an art. We pick partners in the same way we pick a car or an investment. We invest a certain way and we are rewarded. We tend to model ourselves in this same economic principle. Both men and women sell themselves short by looking for the things that are considered attractive in today's market as it relates to fashion and social acceptance. Cultural fashion rather than Godly wisdom can determine what we find attractive as a culture and thus leads to what we find personally acceptable in a mate.

As times have changed so have the laws and theory on love and attraction. At one time, society deemed men who were wild, strong, and maybe a little dangerous to be very appealing. Compare this to the much more modern socially and politically tolerant man we find today. We have allowed secular fashion and secular society to blow the wind that sets the course on our ships of acceptance and attraction. It is my personal opinion that we do not have many men being raised right now in America; we mostly have boys being raised into effeminate, morally vulnerable, and spiritually weak Ken dolls. The church is not off the hook for this reality either...remember it takes a village to raise a child, and this means the men and woman in the church. Our spiritual forefathers had names like "mighty man of valor" or "son of thunder." Those names represent a great identity and masculinity that was established through spiritual forefathers and an intimate relationship with God the Father.

Instead of allowing God and our personal preferences to enter our decision making process as it relates to modern love and choosing a mate, we make choices based on what's popular socially and even on good business sense. When people finally fall in love, in most cases, it is with a mate they believe is the best available choice for them on the market—considering their own value in this process as well. We cannot separate the heart from this process. The heart led by Holy Spirit is our correct compass for such choices. If you want God's best, this is the internal compass that will guide you there.

Chapter two

Separation and Unhealthy Fantasy

One of the most debilitating feelings a human being can feel is separation from God and others. This is the chief goal of satan. If satan can keep us isolated then he can keep us bound, confused, and helpless. It is God's desire that we would not be separated from Him. That is the point of the cross, to draw us to Him in an intimate, covenant relationship. God is accessible to us and thus isolation from God is one of the attributes of hell. If satan can get us living in hell here on earth, then he has stolen the glory and worship from God.

The most common mental illnesses diagnosed worldwide mostly relate to the issue of anxiety. Anxiety itself is the number one diagnosed mental illness in the United States. When we become lonely or feel isolated from others or God we start to see our thinking and actions become defiled with the stains of anxiety. More than likely you at some point in your life have experienced anxiety related to isolation in some form or another. This could be isolation through rejection, poor choices, or abuse. It is a sting that we have all felt and wish to never feel again.

Some of us can easily remember a time when our actions and thoughts were obsessive or destructive due to the issue of anxiety. You can see on the news the stories of anxiety leading to obsession due to fear of separateness. Some people become so gripped with the fear of being abandoned by another person that they let the anxiety drive them to do things that they would never normally do. I want to make this side statement here; there is a fine line between obsession and love, and on a biological level love starts out with a healthy form of obsession, but those feeling are meant to mature into love.

Part of the reason that being separated is such a strong fear for others is due to the fact that it makes you feel vulnerable or helpless to the whims of another. It means that the world around you can invade you at a moment's notice and leave you with no ability to react. Being separate is more like an act that is done to you rather than something that you make a conscious effort to partake in. This reality is what makes this feel so uncontrolled and fearful. Many emotions follow someone who is struggling with separateness. Those emotions vary in intensity from individual to individual.

I had a very close friend who lived under the shadow of shame for several years. I will leave his name out of this but I do have his permission to tell his story. My friend was a member of a very large church and he served at the church in a very small capacity. He would help with basic discipleship and coaching others in study groups. He was also active on the worship team and the prophetic ministry at his church.

One day my friend was telling me about this young lady that he had started dating. He was so excited about what was ahead of him in relation to this new relationship. Unfortunately this friend of mine was involved in a community that was not safe concerning Christian dating and he was made to feel under the microscope which produced a perfect environment for his weakness to come to the surface. My friend and his girlfriend crossed a line sexually and the young man came forward to confess to his leadership team. When he came forward the restoration process was brutal and bloody.

As this event moved on he was asked to leave the church he was serving at and I watched as he fell apart. He wrestled with shame for years after this series of events. Everywhere he went he felt he needed to have a warning label on him. As you can imagine this is so taxing on the human spirit. This was so hard for him to work through. He would just lie on his side and sob for hours in bed. He told me at one point he was averaging 3 hours of sleep a night. My heart went out to him. I have known him since I was a little kid and seeing him like this broke my heart.

For years he wrestled with rejection, blame, anger, and isolation. This was a dangerous place for him to be. I know if his family wasn't near him he would not have made it out alive from the deep level of shame he felt. I remember some nights that were close call for him. It was the only time I had heard him speaks about killing himself to end the pain. He pulled through thank God and is now doing so well and God is blessing his life. It is so refreshing to see him smile and watch what God is doing in him.

One of the most common feelings associated with separateness is shame. Shame is an invisible prison that can keep us bound for as long as our eyes are blind to its door and frame. Shame is something that God never meant for us to feel, but through our fallen nature we are at some point destined to face. Shame is an ugly beast and it is only through the truth of Christ Jesus and the Holy Spirit that we can stand against such spiritual and emotional attacks from the enemy.

The affects of shame can easily be seen in the story of Adam and Eve. In Genesis, they both eat of the tree of good and evil and they both have their eyes opened. They all of a sudden understand what they have done and they have full revelation on their current condition. As soon as they hear God walking in the garden they become afraid and attempt to hide from Him. When we hide in our sin, it simply begets more sin. We never become healed and well through hiding our true selves from God. It is only though letting God love us in our sin that we get victory in that area of our lives.

As Adam and Eve hid in the garden, they felt shame for the first time. The unfortunate thing about living in a world that is fallen is the fact that when Adam did this it shot straight down our family line. We are constantly fighting against the bloodguilt of Adam through the redemptive blood of Christ. Just as death came through one man for all, now through one man we have eternal life. Our spirits are seated with Christ Jesus in heavenly places. However, our souls are being transformed on a daily basis. This means that we will wrestle with the fallen nature in our mind, will, and emotions until we are made perfect at Christ's return.

Shame is not the same thing as conviction. When evaluating the circumstances you are going through it is always good to look at the fruit of it. For instance, if you feel conviction from the Holy Spirit and respond with obedience, changing the way you think and turning from your behavior, then you will experience freedom and power. However, if you are apologizing out of a religious obligation due to your understanding that what you have done is wrong—then the fruit will be shame, self-condemnation, and self-inflicted punishment. When we feel shame we feel defeated and when we feel convicted we feel strength to overcome.

Man was made to dwell in community with other men and this is a biblical, biological, and scientific fact. We were made for communion with God and other human beings, as well as communion with all of creation. To be aware of your own separation from God and others, without the hope of reconciliation and communion through love, is the source of all shame. We are all in a battle. Mankind is in a constant struggle to overcome our separation from the object of our affection and desire. If we allow it, this separation can be wrongly bridged with unhealthy fantasy.

Fantasy is often the catalyst for the things we either subconsciously or consciously believe we are missing in our lives. These are the things that we are often not sure how to get fulfilled. Examples of this would be people who lean on infidelity, gossip, or pornography because they feel they are lacking things in their personal lives. This often gets blamed on a spouse rather than the individual realizing that it is a deeper heart issue. Once we have entertained that fantasy it can get a life of its own and we are left with more than we bargained for. Fantasy, as it relates to psychology, is an imagined or conjured up sequence fulfilling a psychological or emotional need.

Richard Niolon, PhD, writes on the subject of fantasy as well and its worth noting here in my book. I found this section off of his website which you can find in the back of the book in the cited material section. "Fantasy can be a good or a pathological defense. Fantasizing involves creating an inner world when the real world becomes too painful, difficult, or stressful. Thinking about your upcoming vacation when work gets stressful is a healthy use of fantasy. However, if you don't solve problems but only daydream about them being solved for you, if you avoid potentially problematic responsibilities and only fantasize about having rewarding challenges and experiences, fantasy becomes too much."

It is easy to get caught up in fantasy because it is often considered safe and removes the fear of performance or expectations. Fantasy frequently has to do with creating an idealized image of yourself. This is an egocentric behavior and is birthed in pride and self-worship. Our fear of rejection or confrontation can lead us to choose fantasy over reality. How many times have you had an encounter with someone who was a cashier or complete stranger who was rude and then did nothing, but later you began to fantasies of the things you would say or do to that individual? We often feel weak and powerless. This is the breeding ground for broken fantasy, which is the onramp for sin. First comes the temptation, then the invitation to fantasize which can lead to a sinful act.

We must be sober-minded when it comes to the life we give to temptation. Satan has a real plan and the field of this battle is in our minds first and foremost. If we can remain in our minds in a fantasy world then we will not live in our present lives. We must become present and not become numb and inward focused. I have counseled many young men who have felt the sting of rejection and wounding in a sexual relationship and because of unresolved issues. They are in the perfect environment for fantasy and delusion to rule in their own lives and relationships.

Fantasy is a type of defense mechanism. Defense mechanisms are psychological mechanisms aimed at reducing anxiety. This is why fantasy is so accessible. It protects and numbs you when you feel anxiety; even though once you have acted out on your fantasy you are left with an even higher sense of anxiety then when you originally started out. Fantasy can easily become a substitute for addressing the underlying cause and can lead to additional problems. The solution, therefore, is to address the underlying causes of the pain these mechanisms are used to defray.

Fantasy begins to become a place of hiddenness where we hide ourselves from those around us. Just like Golem from Lord of the Rings we have another half we struggle against because we have chosen to hide away a part of ourselves and we are full of broken fantasy. Golem is a character from the Tolkien book "Lord of the Rings" who has been transformed by the power of the ring. He has two personalities one good and one very evil. He is always trying to protect his plan to retrieve the ring with his evil side. He lashes out at anything that gets near his "precious". We protect what we believe is most precious and often times what we find most precious is ourselves. Proverbs 18:1 reminds us, "Whoever isolates himself seeks his own desire; he breaks out against all sound judgment."

Unhealthy fantasy produces bitter fruit. Often times a lack of something we feel we need can become an obsession. We begin to have an idea that someone or something else will fulfill us in a way our spouse or current success won't be able to. We think that "If I could only be with her or him my life would be so much better." I once heard a man say, "Whoever you marry is 80% your perfect match, but then we see someone else with that 20% we are missing and we think that they will be better for us than who we are with now. Once you get into that relationship and lose your kids and your wife you discover that the person you chose is only 20% of what you need." (that is Tyler Perry by the way) Because we tend to live in broken fantasy, we have eyes that do not see correctly.

Often times when you give into your broken fantasies you are left alone and hidden. If you are not careful it can drive you into madness! When we try to live in our broken fantasies it's kind of like drinking salt water or only eating protein; you starve to death while still consuming your deception.

Young girls frequently get their ideas about what beauty is from society. Living in the broken fantasy world this creates can lead to self-esteem and body issues. Some women and girls will throw up to attain that broken fantasy. Even if we don't have an eating disorder like bulimia or anorexia, we can suffer from a similar condition. We are often looking at our lives through fun house mirrors, totally dissatisfied with what we see. We share the same skewed perspective when our vision is not baptized by the Holy Spirit.

Here are the five main types of behaviors from Richard Niolon, PhD, that go along with escaping into unhealthy fantasy. If we use some defenses for too long, they start to happen automatically, separating us from our true feelings.

1. **Displacement** -- One way to avoid the risk associated with feeling unpleasant emotions is to displace them, or put them somewhere other than where they belong. A common example is being angry at your boss. Displaying that anger could cost you your job. You might be afraid that you cannot contain it, but also afraid of what will happen if you express it toward your boss. You might instead express it, but redirect it toward

some other, safer source, such as your partner or best friend. You yell at them and pick a fight. They will forgive you or ignore it, and then you are able to express your anger but without risking your job.

Related to displacement is sublimation, or the healthy redirection of an emotion. Instead of punching your boss when angry with him, instead of taking out your anger on your friends, you go to the gym and punch a punching bag. Other examples include turning the painful loss of a child into a campaign to increase child safety laws, turning a generally high degree of aggression into professional football, and turning the pain and resentment of a physical injury into a drive to overcome a disability.

2. **Projection** -- Projection is something we all do. It is the act of taking something of ourselves and placing it outside of us, onto others; sometimes we project positive and sometimes negative aspects of ourselves. Sometimes we project things we don't want to acknowledge about ourselves, and so we turn it around and put it on others (i.e., "It's not that I made a stupid mistake, it's that you are critical of everything I do!"). The problem with projecting negative aspects of ourselves is that we still suffer under them. In the above example, instead of feeling inadequate (our true feeling) we suffer with the feeling that everyone is critical of us. While we escape feelings of inadequacy and vulnerability, we nonetheless still suffer and feel uneasy.

3. Rationalization -- Rationalization is often called the "sour grapes defense." This comes from one of Aesop's fables. The fox wanted some grapes, but could not reach them. This caused him to feel pain, as he could not have what he wanted. He rationalized, "They were probably sour anyway" to turn them into something he didn't really want, and thus couldn't really be upset about not getting. It is an intellectual way to diminish pain or guilt. The old "They're 50% less fat so I can eat twice as many" routine is the same. You make up a "logical" argument to avoid guilt.

4. Intellectualization -- Related to rationalization, intellectualization involves removing the emotion from emotional experiences, and discussing painful events in detached, uncaring, sterile ways. Someone who intellectualizes becomes very distant from their feelings, and when asked to describe their feelings may find it difficult. They may understand all the words that describe feelings, but have no idea what they really feel.

5. Withdrawal -- Withdrawal is a more severe form of defense. It entails removing yourself from events, stimuli, interactions, etc... that could remind you of painful thoughts and feelings. Withdrawal takes several forms, such as silence, running away, and drinking and drug use. Talking to friends could prompt them to ask about painful events, so you avoid them. Television, books, coworkers, etc... can all remind you of unpleasant feelings, so you avoid them. Paired with fantasy, it can be paralyzing. Withdrawal inevitably leads to strong feelings of loneliness and alienation, however, which generally means you feel more pain.

Fantasy in and of itself is not a bad thing. Fantasy can be a profound tool when it is used creatively for the Kingdom of God. Many writers, artists, and musicians live in a creative place that requires the ability to fantasize and daydream about God. When we subject our imaginations to the Holy Spirit our minds become renewed and our ability to "dream big" can change the world around us. We can break the destructive cycle of unhealthy fantasy by filling our minds and hearts with the Word, prayer, and worship. The only way to combat this type of delusion is through the power of the Holy Spirit and by filling our hearts with a real relationship with the Father.

Chapter three

Identity and Forgiveness

I have found myself charged by the Lord as of late to call the church into a place of hope, identity, and breakthrough. Many in the body of believers are dealing with great grief, and are looking to their past and letting hurts, failures, and mistakes determine where they go in the future. God is committed to us coming into a place where we align ourselves with our true identities as children of God. God desires to give us good gifts, to bless us, and to give us a future.

God wants us to be healed from our painful history and to find our identity in Jesus. The "issues" that make up who we are and how we live are found in how we relate to our past and what we think of Jesus. Finding the grace in God to overcome our past is the key to what will unlock our hearts to move forward with wholeness. The Holy Spirit will reveal the places where we are held captive by bitterness, anger, and shame.

I can remember a time in my life when I was struggling with some major issues in life. They were some real "deal breakers" concerning my walk with the Lord. It is so easy when dealing with wounded thinking to get your focus off of Jesus and off of who you are created to be. It's a bit of a riddle to be honest. We become more inward focused when pacifying hidden wounds. Yet, we lose ourselves in the issues we struggle with. It's like drinking salt water. The more you pacify your wounds the further you get from who you are in Christ. You drink but die of thirst.

When we focus on our past failures and disappointments, it becomes easy to come into agreement with deception. Deception is when we believe a lie about ourselves or God. Both forms of deception produce the same fruit...and that is delusion—a control based way of achievement. We look at our wound and we are not sure that God is good or that God is aware of our pain. Overwhelmed with disappointment, we begin to control our path to destiny. Rather than getting to destiny, we end up on the path of delusion.

The key to unlocking our destiny is to lean on our identity in Christ. One day when I was in prayer and talking with Holy Spirit He said this phrase to me, "Low self-esteem is the number one killer of pastors." In my study I have found that low self-esteem dictates our path to delusion. Understanding our true identity empowers us to walk down the path to our true destiny. When we don't feel like we are enough for God or pleasing to God, we begin to doubt our self worth. Our vision becomes skewed and we start to feel the need to make ourselves valuable rather than believing that we are valuable to the Lord.

I have learned that as you focus more on the ways you fail you begin to lose yourself. The deceptions you have about yourself and God will pervert your dreams and hopes. Destiny is God's dreams for your life and delusion is based on our pain and disappointments. The unresolved wounds we have feed our delusion and steer us off the path of destiny.

Our identity must first be established in our relationship with God. Our relationship with God is grounded as we encounter His thoughts and affections toward us. You have to know that your current circumstances are not punishment for some way you have failed God. If we have a confident relationship with Papa, we will not be waiting for the other shoe to drop, but instead we will overcome the negative aspects of our history and start to walk in confidence and with purpose. If we agree with Heaven and literally start declaring biblical truths about who we are before God, we will begin to soften and become accessible for healing.

One time the Holy Spirit walked me through a vision where I saw a large group of people lined up in front of me. The Holy Spirit showed me how He literally went into each person's past. In one instance, the Holy Spirit went in through the eyes of a woman in front of me. He took me to this woman's bedroom when she was a child. She was lying on her side, crying in bed, and I watched as Holy Spirit started to cup His hands around her feet and breathed into His hands. This little girl started to slowly light up with a warm glow as if light was coming from inside of her and glowing through her skin. I was then pulled back in front of this grown woman. Tears were rolling down her face as she said, "I forgive you, dad." The Holy Spirit had literally gone back in time to when she was an abused little girl, and He healed that place in her heart.

Next, I saw an older man standing in line. Again I went on a journey with Holy Spirit and saw a much younger version of this man sitting on his sofa, sobbing. His wife was explaining to him that she didn't love him anymore and was leaving him for another man. The man was left alone sobbing on his sofa as she said goodbye. Then I watched as Holy Spirit rushed to him and started to put His hands around this young man's heart and breathe. The same event took place as above, and I saw this young man with a warm glow. Then again, I was pulled back and saw the older man now with tears rolling down his face. The man was looking straight forward and said, "I forgive you, sweetheart."

This was what was taking place with everyone in line. They were all allowing the Holy Spirit to go deep into their pain, hurts, and disappointments to heal them. God then said, "I am literally going back in time for the sake of your future." He gave me a vision of everyone in the line standing with luggage in their hands. At the front of the line was an airplane. Written on the side of the airplane was the phrase, "Acceleration" I heard a voice in Heaven say, "If you're boarding the promises of God, you have to check your baggage." The luggage was too big and heavy to take on board this airplane of acceleration and had to be handed over to Jesus before boarding. As people chose to hand the luggage over to Jesus, He took their baggage from them.

We need to let go of the baggage in our lives and move forward with Him. God is dedicated to us going into our future—healed up and restored. Let's choose to be brave and allow the Holy Spirit to go into our past so we can be made whole and released into our future! Make a decision today to not hold captive those past wounds and failures, but to trust Jesus with our past, present, and future. Today the Father wants us to choose to forgive.

I want you, the reader, to literally pray, "Father, I trust You and give You permission to go into the deep places of my past and do a work of healing. I forgive those who may have hurt me out of ignorance or even malice and I choose to give them to You. I give You (person's name) and everything that this person did to me. Lord, please forgive them. I invite You, Holy Spirit, to even now begin a work in my heart toward daily forgiveness. I choose to let these past hurts go for the sake of my future. In the name of Jesus, Amen."

Chapter four

Loving God with All You Are

Jesus said, "You shall love the Lord your God with all your heart, with all your soul, with your entire mind, and with all your strength." (Mark 12:30) Now, God created us to love Him in these four spheres of our life. Heart, soul, mind, and strength are each distinct spheres of our life. They do overlap, but they are distinct. The reason God created us to love Him in this way is because this is the way He loves us. Can you imagine that God loves you with all His mind? You can look up into the sky on a starry night and see the vast universe and the vastness of God's mind. God says, "I love you with all My mind and that is why I want you to love Me with all your mind." Now, love does not automatically develop in these four distinct spheres of life without our involvement. We have an involvement in each one of them and they are distinctly different.

In Matthew 22, Matthew added another sentence to Jesus' statement which Mark omitted. It is in verse 38 (paraphrased). Jesus added, "This is the first commandment and this is the great commandment." It is the first commandment, because it is God's first priority. It is the first emphasis of the Holy Spirit in your life. If you are paying attention to the Spirit and you are actually receiving His direction, I assure you the first thing He is emphasizing is that you should love God in these four ways. That is always first on His agenda. It is the thing He is doing first in the church. It is not only the first commandment, it is the great one. It has the greatest impact on God's heart. It is the one commandment that impacts God the most. It moves His heart and it impacts our heart. It impacts the hearts of the people we love in the overflow of loving God.

Loving God with all you are does not just have the greatest impact, but it is the greatest calling. I have talked to many people through the years who are anxious about discovering God's will for their life. They are really stirred about this and it is a good thing to be stirred about it. When you ask them about the will of God for their life, they are mostly focused on what are they supposed to do. But the will of God for your life—although it does involve this for sure—is first what you are supposed to become, not what you are supposed to do. When I meet someone and he says, "I am struggling to find the will of God," I am thinking, "I already know the main will of God for your life: the first commandment. It is the first priority." People primarily focus on what they are supposed to do, and God does care about that, but what we are supposed to become is more important and this needs to capture our understanding, our mind.

Let's start by examining how to love God with all our heart. We are to love God in a way that involves and touches our emotions. It is not just a cold, distant, obedient, dutiful servant hood. It is not that we are involved in a program of ministering to people in a dutiful and responsible way. We are to love God in a way that effects and stirs our emotions. I am not talking about emotionalism. I am not talking about stirring us up, but I am talking about consciously doing what is in the Word of God, which increases our desire for God.

The Bible makes it clear that we have a significant role in determining how our emotions develop over time. Some imagine that whatever happens in their emotions just happens, but I want to tell you that you have a significant involvement in the development of your emotions and of how you feel. It takes a while to change your emotions, but you can change them. Our emotions will follow whatever we set ourselves to pursue. If you set yourself to pursue something, your emotions will take hold of it the longer you pursue it. It is just how the human spirit works.

When Jesus said, "Love Me with all your heart," He meant, "Love Me in a way that causes your emotions to take hold of Me and to connect with Me." It is within the reach of every human to do that. In Psalm 91:14, God talks about the person who sets his love on God. If we set our love on Him, our desire for love will increase. We need to make it an object of focus, go after it, and not just say, "Well, I love God kind of on the way, you know. Sure, I love God in a general sense." That is not enough. We need to set our love on Him and say, "Lord, I want my heart and my emotions to be engaged in my pursuit of You." Again, I am not talking about how we express our emotions in a meeting. I am talking about the way our heart engages with God. As you change your mind, the Spirit will change your emotions. You have power to change your mind, and the Spirit will change your emotions according to what you do with your mind. Some folks say, "I just grit my teeth and change my emotions." How does that work? You set your mind on pursuing things and your emotions will follow in time.

The second sphere is loving God with all our mind. We do this by filling our mind with that which inspires love for God instead of filling it with that which diminishes love for God. Our mind is the doorway to our inner man. What we do with our mind greatly affects our capacity to love. If we fill our minds with the right things, our capacity to love increases. If we fill our mind with wrong things, our capacity to love diminishes. Much of our life and even most of our life actually occurs in our mind. Maybe that is a strange idea, but most of your life occurs in your mind.

Your mind is going 24 hours a day. It never stops. It is not supposed to stop. It never will. It is designed that way. Your mind will be actively going 24 hours a day, for billions of years. There is never a time that your mind stops, never. The language of the human spirit is images, it is pictures. That is the language of your spirit. If I say, "Pink elephant," you do not just think of the concept. You instantly picture a pink elephant. Our mind is an internal movie screen that continually shows pictures. It is always running and it will run forever. It will never stop. When you sleep, you recognize a fraction of one percent of the images. We call those dreams, but you are never aware of the vast majority of the images.

Your mind is like a vast universe within. You will be learning and remembering things for billions of years and you will never exhaust the capacity of your mind in the resurrection. In this age there are so many layers in the natural mind. We cannot recall most of what is in that big hard drive called "the human mind." It is a vast universe. It can never be turned off, never. For billions of years, the images can never be shut down, but they can be directed. The images can be changed. We can replace the dark thoughts with new ones. We can rewrite the movie script which plays on the inside. We can rewrite it. Now, it is interesting that we are the producer, we are the main star, and we are the consumer in that movie script. We produce it, we act in it, and we watch it. We are both the hero and the villain in all our movies, and some others are involved as well. This is kind of funny, but it is actually true.

The reason I am saying this, is that with the vast influential power of the mind, it is amazing that so many believers are so casual about what they do with their mind. The mind is this glorious and powerful reality that has vast potential. So many believers fill their minds with entertainment and waste time daydreaming about vanity. This is disheartening because they have the Holy Spirit and a Bible and the Kingdom of God. The Lord is saying, "Love Me with your mind. Do not fill your mind with so much entertainment and do not be so absorbed in daydreaming about vanity. Take hold of the reins of your mind. Read the Word of God. Love Me with your mind."

Sphere number three is loving God with our strength. To love God with all our strength refers to our natural strength and our natural resources. Our natural resources are more than just money. They are our time, our physical energy, and our words. Now, we express love for God by the way we choose to invest our resources. When we give God our strength or our resources, we express our love for God in a way that is meaningful to Him and in a way He cares about. Again, I am not talking about money only. I am talking about all our strength. God takes that personally. He takes it as an act of love, because it is costly for us to give our resources to Him. It costs us something. We lose something in the natural when we give our resources to Him. Now, He always returns them. He multiplies them and returns them, but for that moment we actually lose them. We do this because we love Him and He takes it personally. He smiles and He says, "I like that."

It says in Hebrews 6:10 (paraphrased), that God will not forget the love you show towards Him when you do things for other people. You are actually showing love to Him and He sees it that way. Now, the normal thing to do for all human beings is to use our resources to increase our personal comfort and our personal honor. We use our time, we use our money, and we use our words to obtain more honor and to get more things coming our way. There is nothing wrong with that. We are supposed to do this, but we are not supposed to use *all* our strengths that way. Part of our strength we are to give away. We are to sow it with a view to loving God. We give it away and we actually lose it temporarily, because we love Him and He receives it as a statement of love.

Every time we invest our strength into our relationship with Him or into His purposes, He sees it. Now, when we sow our time, when we sow our money, when we sow our physical energy, we are sowing it into God's bank, so to speak. God takes careful record of it, He records it, He notes it, He remembers it, He esteems it, He values it, and then He returns it to us, but multiplied. You give God your time and I assure you that when you give God your time, you are giving Him a chance to increase your influence. When you are giving Him your time you are giving Him some of your effectiveness and your productivity.

2 Corinthians 12:9 is the verse I consider the principle of the fasted lifestyle. This is the main principle and main verse I use when I think of the fasted lifestyle. Paul is suffering persecution and he is pained over it. People are speaking wrong things about him, lies about him. He is getting beaten with whips. He is being put in prison. People are undermining his ministry and hindering his money. Every time he turns around, something is coming against him, and the Lord appears to him and says in effect, "Paul, let Me explain something to you. My grace is sufficient for you, because My strength will be perfected in you as you continue in weakness" (v.9, paraphrased). That is an interesting phrase.

Now, the weakness the Lord is talking about is not moral weakness. He is not saying, "As you keep sinning and seeking forgiveness, you will see how nice I am." That is true. You do see how nice God is when He forgives you and He forgives me, but Paul is not talking about moral weakness here. He is talking about voluntarily embracing weakness in the choices he is making. It means that if he walks into a specific city and preaches, he is going to get beaten up. He knows it. He is going to get hit with rods, but he walks in, he preaches, and they beat him. He comes back and it is as if he says, "Ah, I am just really set back. I am in pain. I cannot minister for a while." In other words, he voluntarily embraces weakness in terms of his productivity and strength. And the Lord may say, "You wait and see what I will do."

Another way of pouring yourself out is prayer. I give up a couple of hours of my time—my time is my productivity—to sit in a room and tell God what He tells me to tell Him. You say, "God, I can do more." God says, "No, give Me your productivity, your time. You tell Me what I tell you to tell Me." That is pouring out, because I am giving my strength away. You tithe your money. You give ten percent and go beyond that and give another ten percent. When you give your money, you are giving your strength and your ability of influence. You actually really lose it. When you give one hundred dollars, that one hundred dollars is really gone. It is as if the Lord says, "In My accounting system, I will return the financial strength you have lost. I will return what you have lost in productivity by giving Me your time. I will return everything back to you in My timing."

When we pour out what God has already put inside of us it is the context in which God releases His strength. When He says, "My grace is sufficient for you," the word grace has two components. There is a mercy dimension of grace, which is unmerited favor. God forgives you.

We talk about His grace and often we mean His mercy or His willingness to give us unmerited favor. We do not deserve it, but we get it. There is a mercy dimension to grace, but there is a bigger dimension to grace than mercy. Mercy is a sub-unit of grace. The other dimension of grace, which is what it mostly means, is God's enabling or God's empowering in your life. So, the Lord is not saying, "My forgiveness for you is sufficient." He is saying in effect, "My enabling of you is sufficient. If you will embrace leaning on your beloved, you will see a greater enabling. You will see a greater increase called perfected strength."

We fast our strength in five main ways as taught by Jesus in the Sermon on the Mount. The five main areas are by serving, by giving money, by praying—because that is an investment of time—and by blessing our adversaries, by speaking words of blessing instead of speaking words to settle the score, to get even. Instead of speaking words to put our adversaries in place, we bless them, we speak opposite words. The fifth way is by fasting food. Fasting food is not really about hunger. It may seem that way if you are new at fasting. Fasting is mostly about physical weakness. I mean, you are hungry for a day or two when you fast. You are always hungry a little bit, but the compelling hunger lifts.

The far bigger problem with fasting is that you are emotionally, mentally, and physically wobbly. As I go on different fasts, I say, "Lord, I have work to do. I cannot pay attention. I am staring. I am making a handout. I am writing the same sentence ten times. Lord, I have the Friday night meeting in one hour. I cannot make it work." It is as if the Lord says, "Stay with it. Stay with the fasting." Fasting is physical weakness. We do not have the same ability; we do not have that clarity of mind. Our emotions get wobbly, our mind is wobbly, and our body is wobbly. We really give our strength to the Lord when we do that.

But, when you fast, do not measure it in months. Measure it in years and you will have far greater productivity when you look back over ten years. God really does take it into account. Serving people is a form of fasting and this is a prime example of needing the filter of the Holy Spirit to view and serve others. When you are serving people, you really lose time and energy. You really could use that same time and that same energy to enrich your life. You give time and energy which you will never get back except that God returns it in His own way later. And He receives it as love. It is as if the Lord says, "I take it very personally that you invested yourself in that way." Now, this is called *loving God with your strength* and He wants us to love Him with our strength. This is different than loving Him with our mind and different than loving Him with our heart.

Now we will go to the final sphere, the fourth sphere: loving God with our soul. When we love God with our soul, this is related to how we derive our identity. How we establish our identity is related to loving God with our soul. Let me explain. Our identity is determined by how we define success and value, by how we see ourselves. The most natural way we define success is by our accomplishments. Or we find our feeling of success in the approval of others. But what the Lord wants us to do is find our identity and our definition of success in our relationship with Him, instead of in our accomplishments or from other people. We all naturally and automatically find our identity in what we accomplish and who recognizes us. It is as if the Lord says, "I want you to go on a journey of shifting in a radical way the way you define success and therefore, the way you derive your identity, the way you see yourself."

This is a foundational point. This is Christianity 101. It is a foundation of which we need to be constantly reminded. God's love for us is what determines our personal worth. The reason I am worth so much, and the reason you are worth so much, is because God chose us and He loves us. In the same way, it is significant that we respond to God's love and love Him in return. That is not a small thing; it is not an automatic thing. Of all the billions of people on the earth, about a billion people—according to the statistics—love God. That leaves about six billion people who do not love God. Now, you are so used to being saved that you think this is not a big deal. No, you are in the significant minority of history. You are one of the minority to whom God said, "I love you," and by the grace of God you said, "I will take it and I will return it. I will love You, too." Beloved, that is what makes your life successful in the most profound sense.

We need to be anchored in the truth that our success and our worth are based on the fact that He loves us and we love Him, instead of it being based on our accomplishments, our recognition, our possessions, and our relationships. Those are the natural ways through which we get our identity: by how much we achieve and who recognizes it. But that is a really broken system. Because of our natural mindset and because of the darkness of our mind, almost everybody's first response—unless they unlearn it—is to feel rejected and neglected by people. The whole human race feels this way. So, if we get our identity by being recognized by people, our default is to feel rejected and neglected and become emotionally damaged in the process. Then our accomplishments seem so small and so unnoticed that we do not like them.

Most people look at their accomplishments and they despise them because they seem so insignificant. They are in a crisis of identity and it creates a storm of emotional traffic on the inside, a constant preoccupation with trying to find some way of feeling valuable. Then, popular culture tells us how to do it with all the fashions and looks and styles. I am not against all that stuff. I am against some of it, but not all of it. The problem is that people can spend their entire lives caught up in that whirlwind and they cannot really connect with God in any way compared to how they would be able to, if they were not living with this identity crisis.

This is a sentence I learned to start saying some time ago when I came under pressure. When you come under pressure it makes you philosophical. I think it makes almost everyone philosophical. You say, "Why am I even doing this anyway?" When pressure hits, it makes us ask big questions. The Genesis 1 God, the only one who has Genesis 1 on His resume, He likes me—the Genesis 1 God. I would say, "You know, that works. Wow." I would get this idea that I have it made. Then the Lord would say, "That is not it. It is not enough that I like you. I want you to respond and to love Me. If I love you and you love Me, you are already successful."

Going through the philosophical questions I could feel the pressure, and the only way I could land with comfort was by saying, "I am loved by God, and I am a lover of God. Therefore, I am already successful. I made it! Everything else is icing on the cake. I have already made it!" Then I would be happy. If you feel successful, the relationships, the money, the difficulties, the problems, and the resistance come into perspective.

Having the correct perspective on our lives is also key to avoiding burnout. Burnout does not come from hard work, but from working with a wrong spirit. You will not get burned out because you work long hours. You get burned out because you are working long hours with a wrong spirit, meaning, you are working to become successful at the heart level. When you work in order to become successful, the work will burn you out. If you work because you already are successful, the work will actually strengthen your spirit. So, if we work from success, we get renewed, but if we work to become successful, we get burned out. I can spend long hours engaged in ministry and I can be involved in difficult problems in people's lives and difficult solutions if, in my core, I already know I am successful. But if I am doing the work so I can prove that I have a ministry, that work will burn me out and I will become disillusioned.

The Lord wants us to shift the way we get our identity. This is how we love God with our soul, so that our identity is in our relationship with Him and not in what we produce with our hands or who recognizes us. It is a journey to make the change and to make that identity shift. It is not a one-day decision. You make the decision one day and then you just go on that journey and you stick with it. I have been on that journey for years and sometimes I lose my way and then I sign back up. I lose my way and I sign back up. I lose my way and I sign back up.

I lose my way, I become philosophical, and the only way I get my comfort is by saying, "I am loved and I am a lover; therefore, I am successful. OK, my problem is not that big, because my spirit is happy now." When you have a right identity it removes so much of the emotional traffic. You can love God far better with a clear spirit. I believe this is what Jesus meant when He said, "Love Me with all your soul."

Chapter five

Revelation on Judgment, Miracles, and Kingdom Living

Judgment is an attribute of God's character and nature so we want to understand judgment as it relates to love and how we relate to those around us. Growing up in western Christianity I have seen and heard many things relating to God's judgment. I have heard everything from God's judgments are punishment to God doesn't judge us at all. This can be a confusing process for young people to go through in church culture. What is the truth about judgment and why does it seem so foggy at times?

Jesus even addresses this issue about being judged in the Bible several times. At one point Jesus says in Luke 13, when addressing those around Him, "Do you think that these Galileans were worse sinners than all the other Galileans, because they suffered in this way?" Jesus was saying all need to repent or perish and that catastrophe doesn't come only to "prove God's point" concerning people we don't agree with. Rather, life simply happens and all should be ready in their hearts.

I am hearing a lot of things as of late on the issue of catastrophe and the wrath of God as it pertains to mankind and the globe. I find myself on a personal journey with the Lord on this issue and on how we respond as the Church. My heart has been gripped over the reaction I have seen and heard concerning Haiti's earthquake and judgment. I am asking the Lord, "Papa, what do You want us to do?" I believe that the Lord has given me specific prophetic insight into such issues as wrath and catastrophes.

On New Year's Eve the Lord spoke a very clear word to me during an event at our church. We had just wound down the celebration into the New Year and were celebrating with a time of worship and prophetic declaration when, all at once, the Lord broke in and spoke to me! I heard the Lord speak this phrase: "I will tug on the heartstrings of this world, and My Church will be the cords of loving kindness. The Church will be My song to this world."

I began to dialog with the Lord by asking, "Papa, what do you mean?" And the Lord spoke to me and said, "There is coming catastrophe to the world and I am providing opportunity for My Church to shine the Light of Christ to the hurting and lost." The Lord started telling me that, "When we observe judgment or wrath, My Bride uses it as a reason to do nothing."

We need to rise as the Church and pray for God to bless and help those who are going through suffering, praying for the glory of God to come. We sometimes make internal statements like, "Well, they are in sin so they deserved what happened to them." The major problem with this kind of thinking is that once we agree with those thoughts, we reject others and do nothing with the opportunity we have just been given.

The Lord spoke and said, "My Church is missing the opportunities that are being laid out before them because they have misunderstood My nature and character." I started asking the Lord to show me what He means by this statement and He began to overwhelm me with His glory and fear. I began to manifest and shake under the weight of His presence. Then the Lord spoke again to me and said, "My Church doesn't understand My nature and character, thus they do not respond correctly; you think you know Me but you do not! My Church thinks I am one-dimensional in My nature and character, thus you only side with one dimension, but I tell you that I will never suspend one attribute for another. I am fully wrath and fully love, fully mercy and fully chastising."

We are called to act on behalf of God on this earth. We have a mandate to be the actions of Christ in this world. We must interpret the times and respond under Holy Spirit unction at a precise moment. The world will be given a "road to Damascus" experience, I believe, and the Church must be poised and ready to be the light of Christ in that moment and speak a word to the lost, dying, and hurting. We must respond in prayer and tenderness to the world around us for the sake of worldwide salvation through God-given opportunity. There is a great harvest coming and the Lord of the Harvest is waiting for us to join up with His work.

I believe that we are entering into a season of great signs and wonders. I have been reading the book of Luke for the past several months and cannot seem to move past the story of the woman with the issue of blood. I feel that we are right now on the cusp of an incredible harvest, with signs and wonders bringing it in and following the harvest around. We are at a precise moment of a great dispensing of the power of God released into the lives of the lost and broken.

Luke 8:43-47: And there was a woman who had had a discharge of blood for twelve years, and though she had spent all her living on physicians, she could not be healed by anyone. She came up behind Him and touched the fringe of His garment, and immediately her discharge of blood ceased. And Jesus said, "Who was it that touched Me?" When all denied it, Peter said, "Master, the crowds surround You and are pressing in on You!" But Jesus said, "Someone touched Me, for I perceive that power has gone out from Me." And when the woman saw that she was not hidden, she came trembling, and falling down before Him declared in the presence of all the people why she had touched Him, and how she had been immediately healed. And He said to her, "Daughter, your faith has made you well; go in peace."

In this story of the woman with the issue of blood, we see a desperate woman who has tried everything up to this point for healing and wholeness. We see a woman who is desperate for a touch. She recognizes the Messiah and pushes through the crowd to touch the fringe of Jesus' garment. She believed that Jesus carried the ability to bring her into wholeness. I believe this is the opportunity that the Church is being given at this moment: to carry the power of Christ into this world unto healing, deliverance, and wholeness to those who are desperate for a touch. We are surrounded by people who are helpless and harassed, and we are to be filled with compassion for those who are not yet reconciled to God.

I was sitting at home with my wife and started meditating on the Scripture from Luke 8, and all at once my heart was filled with compassion and the Holy Spirit began to dialog with me on this very story. The Holy Spirit spoke to me and said, "I am calling in those who have issues and are ready to push through the crowd of their circumstances into the place of true relationship with Jesus. I am finding those who have set themselves aside in the place of desperation for a touch from Jesus. I am reaching out to the lost so they can bring testimony of what I have done for them into the church and out into the world."

The woman with the issue of blood pushed through the crowd in desperation, and she reached out and touched Jesus. When Jesus felt power leaving from Him, He stopped what He was doing so He could address the one who touched Him. There are several reasons that Jesus stopped to recognize the woman for touching Him. I believe one reason is so Jesus could restore her in front of everyone. Had she been healed and not been publicly restored, she would have later been stoned for her actions and for not declaring herself unclean. The other reason I believe that Jesus brought her out in front of everyone was to show her great faith and for her to build faith in others through the sharing of her testimony.

Do you see how this story played out? She pushed through the
crowd because she was desperate and she believed in Jesus as the Messiah. After her faith paid off, she then was recognized before God and men. She fell to her knees when she saw that she could not hide. I felt the Holy Spirit say that the woman went to her knees as a prophetic symbol of the secret place of prayer, and then she began to give her powerful testimony and many watched and were amazed.

Then the Holy Spirit said to me, "This is what I am getting ready to do. I am causing a great awakening where the lost will have an encounter with Me through desperation, and they will bring their testimonies into the church, media and the marketplace, and many will be saved through the power of their testimony."

In order to walk in the fullness of what God has planned for us, it is vital that we understand some of the principles of the Kingdom of God. The things of the Kingdom are not to be studied and absorbed so that we will "have it down" and claim yet another notch on our belt. Rather, the things of the Kingdom of Heaven are things we will spend our entire lives running after and pursuing. Some of us will get a glimpse at this reality and others will never say "yes" to the invitation from God to fully know the Kingdom.

The wonderful thing about the Kingdom of Heaven is that we can walk in it here on earth if we do what it takes to be carriers of the Kingdom. I am not talking about a legalistic approach to authority. I am talking about becoming like Christ. You see, as we are transformed into the likeness of Christ we get His attributes. Our very personalities and emotions get baptized by the blood of Christ, and so we keep our uniqueness and yet we take on a new identity and reality. Jesus has authority and gives us authority based on the cross and relationship. You cannot have one without the other. This is what makes it possible for us to walk in the power of the Kingdom of Heaven.

I have been in a place of prayer for the Western Church and for what the Lord wants to do in this *now* season, and I keep finding that the Holy Spirit is beckoning us to a place of spiritual maturity and wisdom. The Lord wants us to partner with Him in bringing Heaven to earth. We can walk in a supernatural realm right now, here on earth, if we so choose. Many churches are "talking" about Heaven invading earth. But we can attain this reality in a very basic and simple way...the secret is relationship with the Father. When we set ourselves apart in real, intimate relationship with the Father, His presence and glory literally emanate from us. When we acknowledge the presence of God in us and on us, then we become aware of the fruit of personal relationship. We are sowing into our relationship with the Lord and thus we reap the fruit of that relationship.

Peter walked in this kind of a reality with the Lord. People would lay out the sick and dying hoping that even Peter's shadow would hit the people and set them free. Peter brought Heaven to earth through relationship. Jesus set the prime example of this reality for us; by bringing Heaven to earth He made it an accessible reality for all of us. I am consumed, desperate, and hungry for this reality to be a common occurrence in the Western Church. The Holy Spirit spoke to me and said, "It's attainable right now for every believer. We long to send the River all over the Western Church. This river is a real outpouring that breaks forth in signs and wonders. It is irrefutable evidence of the strong working power of the Holy Spirit in your Church and life.

Recently, I was in a service and the minister was talking about the River of God being in the place of worship. I was deep in prayer, just dialoging with the Holy Spirit. As I often do, I asked Holy Spirit about His River being in our midst. The Spirit spoke to me and said, "My son, do you not know that the River is a real, tangible thing? The River of God is made up of the very nature and character of God Himself. Everything in Heaven is from God and of God. We are looking for those who have carved out river beds in their lives through lining up with the nature and character of God—those who have an intimate relationship with Us."

There are so many rewards for those who love God and walk according to His Word, will, and way. We have all things accessible to us who believe. The question is: "Are you setting yourself apart for the Lord?" Because once you walk humbly in relationship with the Lord, Heaven coming down is a matter of your internal life coming forth. There are many who have just charisma, but there are also those who have real power because of being in relationship with Jesus. The Spirit spoke to me and said, "We are not after membership, but rather We are after relationship."

I believe that we are on the twilight of great things in God, but we must be wise virgins (Mathew 25:1-13) and make sure that we are prepared for what is coming. We must allow the Holy Spirit to carve out a foundation in our character to receive the character and nature of Jesus. We want to be a place where His presence can rest and manifest itself in us and through us.

Chapter six

Young Lessons on Love

Looking back over my life I am surprised as I spend time with the Lord how much He has allowed me to see and just how much He Himself has inspired and healed me concerning these old graves and cradles. Old graves meaning my past that I hadn't truly released myself from and cradles meaning immaturity that I the Lord is working to full maturity. As I am now on this journey to giving and receiving love in my own life, I have become inspired that it is the path to being a dispenser of the Kingdom. We should never forget where we came from and always have in the front of our minds our destiny in Christ Jesus. I know some people need to move past their own history of mistakes, but I implore you—do not forget what He has saved you from so that you might have freedom and eternal life.

I was recently meditating on how my life started out, growing up in a sleepy little town called Minot, North Dakota. I was replaying my childhood and the area of town I grew up in—as well as the motley crew of messy faced, bike riding vigilantes I grew up with. The kids I grew up with have become totally unique and beautiful adults. Some have been dealt bad cards in life that is for sure. Yet, some have carved out for themselves a way out of the small town and the snow to find their version of happiness.

All this thought of my childhood put me in a place where I had to think about how I learned what love is. I would like to tell you I learned what love was from growing up in the Church and reading my Bible. This was not the case. A side note here is that the Church should be the one to teach people about love and what love looks like. It would save a lot of heartache in people if the Church wasn't so afraid to speak into this sometimes awkward and uncomfortable area of people's lives. The Church must come back into place where it does some mothering and fathering—not in a legalistic, opinionated way, but rather in wisdom, love, and biblical truth.

I remember one of the first lessons in love for me came in the form of a little Vietnamese girl who was a grade school classmate of mine. She and her family lived down the street from me and I would get so excited at the thought of going and playing with my Vietnamese friends. I loved going over to their house because their mom would always make us traditional Vietnamese food. For a middle class white kid from North Dakota, that was about as good as it gets! Now this "love," which was really nothing more than an innocent crush on my classmate, was one of the first lessons I learned about what love is.

On our street we had characters that I will never forget. We had a few blocks that we owned (in our young little opinions) and these streets were the backdrop for this first lesson on love. See, at the end of our street we had these two sisters who were alcoholics.

They were old and mean, with an equally mean old dog that my classmates and I were thoroughly convinced had supernatural powers. This dog was like a giant bellowing mystery because even though it would bark and shake, there was plywood covering the windows so we never really could see the dog. We were, however, convinced in our young minds that this demon hound had consumed many children from our neighborhood (I am being colorful, of course).

I would often have to walk by the beat up shack that these two sisters lived in, the sisters we so lovingly referred to as the "drunk ladies." If I wanted to see my Vietnamese classmate and eat the bounty of her family's kitchen, then I would have to pass by "The House" to get there. I remember the feeling of getting butterflies in my stomach, thinking about if that dog ever got out while I was walking, or if the drunk ladies ever got a hold of me, what might happen? I would stand a little ways down the street and work up the courage and run as fast as I could past this gauntlet of danger to see the girl I was sweet on. So, I learned a lesson even at that age that love means having to be brave. I know it may sound cute, but it really has been a valuable lesson for me when I face hard circumstances and think about the reward for bravery in the face of hardships...a warm bowl of Vietnamese soup (ha-ha). But seriously, the reward for being brave is the power to overcome again and again.

It seemed like the Church didn't offer these kinds of lively, raw, and beautiful feelings. At least I wasn't being taught about them. I know for sure we didn't talk about these kinds of feelings in Sunday school. Maybe we should have though? The Church I grew up in and the Church that I see today, as a whole, is scared to death of feelings. I don't get it! So many Christians are walking around constantly repressing their feelings because in their hearts they believe that God is repulsed by their feelings and emotions. He is not. God gave you your personality and emotions. When you became reconciled through Christ, your emotions were baptized under the blood of Jesus Christ. This means that your emotions are not a hindrance anymore, but rather an asset for your good and fulfillment.

You will live out of more boldness, power, and longevity in the Kingdom if you embrace who Christ is in you and all that He has made in you as well. He knit you in your mother's womb, which means He knit every aspect of you and your personality—not just your physical appearance. Most of the people I knew in Church would love to quote scripture like this one, "The human heart is inherently wicked," (Jeremiah 17:9) and then they would follow up with some outrageous statement like, "You can never trust your emotions because they are wicked." The truth is that we need to constantly lay our bodies, minds, and spirits before the Lord and allow the Holy Spirit to bring about change in us. Having feelings and admitting when something hurts or coming to terms with the fact that you are disappointed does not mean your feelings are wicked. The verse quoted above is actually in reference to an unredeemed heart, not the heart of someone who is now filled with the heart and mind of Christ Jesus.

To look for God in our lives and let our experiences show us areas of ourselves is to be present and awake in this life. This is so much better than sleepwalking around in this world thinking that life just happens to us. This kind of numb living is what haunts a man at the end of his life. The thought that we were never emotionally present with our loved ones or that we really never made an impact in the lives of those we love is frightening. I have spoken with generals of the faith who are at the twilight of their lives and many have the same deep regret…that they were not truly present in their lives and circumstances. To be present in this life means to be fully alive, hearts beating wild and free, and emotions fully baptized by the Holy Spirit. The most dangerous kind of Christians are those who enjoy God and live their lives accordingly in this world.

While we walk this earth, the lessons regarding what it truly means to love are some of the most meaningful. The loss of a close friend, early in my life, taught me a lot about what it means to love. It was the summer of my sixth grade year and I was a rambunctious kid growing up in a middle class neighborhood. As a child, the summer was what I lived for. All my friends pretty much fit the same mold, in the sense of being fun-loving kids. At this point in my life, I'd never experienced the loss of anyone close to me. One day, I remember my parents introducing me to a young man named Adam. My parents knew his family through some friends at the church I grew up in.

I still remember the first time I met Adam. I could tell something was different about this young man. He looked different then the other friends I had. I remember him being such a sweet kid, really tender and kind. But Adam was the first friend I ever had who was dealing with a disease. Most of my friends were relatively healthy kids with no real health problems, so meeting someone who was sick was not the norm for me. I spent quite a few summer nights hanging out with Adam and I learned a lot from that short friendship. The Lord used it to teach me something about love.

See, we tend to be scared of people when we know that they're sick, mostly because we're afraid of losing them. It's always a risk and a gamble to love someone. To extend friendship to someone involves an element of risk and trust. It can be difficult to relate to people who are sick due to our own lack of education, fear, bias, or prejudice. Oftentimes we don't understand what having an illness can do to people, both mentally and emotionally, and so we forget things like empathy, compassion, patience, and positivity. It is Christ to think outside of yourself for the benefit of serving others in a place of great need.

In studying psychology you learn that people tend to reject the people and situations they don't understand. This is mostly due to fear and not out of an innate cruelty that we as human beings have. I find people lash out at what they are afraid of and that includes sickness. Sometimes the thought process can go something like this: "If you are sick or dying, then that means that same thing can happen to me. I could become sick and die, and then what would happen to those I love?" We, as human beings, become fearful when we are confronted with the fact that we are but a vapor and we will tenaciously do whatever it takes to get as far away from that reality as possible. We push sick people away because we are fearful of our own mortality.

Christ has called us to not be bound by fear, but rather to heal the sick and embrace loving one another as family. Imagine, if you have children, that your child is sick...would you just leave them in a room and forget about them? Or would your compassion be aroused fully for them, thus causing you to embrace them so they don't have to feel scared or alone? How many of you have felt scared and alone and would do anything to feel a touch? These are the kinds of questions the Holy Spirit is asking you concerning loving those who are sick, desperate, broken, and dying. Will you love them or push them away out of selfish fear?

Adam was the kind of invitation from the Lord that I could have just blown off and never looked back. Honestly, I could have just refused to go over and hang out with Adam because it was different and awkward for me due to my lack of understanding. Adam had cancer and did not have long to live. I didn't fully understand it at the time, but I have now gleaned so much beauty from that friendship. I learned that love is not about reward, but about something much greater. Love is an open hand, an ongoing giving motion that is always overflowing. This kind of love is the love of Christ Jesus. There have been so many times in my life I have seen Him in these life lessons. Jesus is real and His DNA is all around us if we open our eyes. His very attributes are manifested in our lives and the lives around us.

There was one particular evening that stands out in my mind. I was spending the night at my pastor's house with Adam. At the time, he was going through chemotherapy and was completely bald. I remember finally just talking to him about it all. I asked questions that would have been offensive if I hadn't been a totally naive child. I remember that Adam had a particular smell to him when he was going through treatment. To this day, I haven't forgotten that smell. Sometimes when I am in a hospital I can still smell that medicinal smell and my mind goes back to my sixth grade summer and Adam. The night that I spoke with Adam he let me look at his portable IV and feel his bald head. Adam had lost all of his hair from the chemotherapy and his head was soft and smooth. I asked Adam if he was afraid he was going to die. He looked at me and said, "Yes, I am afraid." I had never been exposed to such heart rending conversation in my young life. I remember crying with Adam, afraid for him and what his future looked like.

Soon after our conversation, Adam and his family left to go back home to Arizona. I didn't hear from him for awhile. Then, during the beginning of my seventh grade year, I came home one night from a dance at my school and my parents asked me to sit down at the table in the kitchen. I could feel that something wasn't right. My stomach began to turn due to the things I was picking up on in my spirit. My dad and mom said, "Honey, there is something we need to tell you...Adam died today." I remember crying so hard at the kitchen table for the loss of my friend. This was the first time I had ever experienced the loss of someone close to me.

My friend Ronnie is another guy who helped me learn a little more about love. Several years ago, I lived with a sweet family in Minot that moved from Seattle, Washington to North Dakota. They were an awesome family, full of love, very human, and impressively brave. I was going through some hard times and I lived in their basement. This was during my prodigal years when I was still working out my drug addiction and wrong ideas about the Lord. I have to admit those were some beautiful times for me relating to understanding love.

This family also had a young man named Ronnie who they provided in home care for. Ronnie lived with this family and was severely mentally and physically disabled. If I remember correctly, doctors said he had the understanding of a seven-year-old. He was actually 15 at the time, I believe. Ronnie was an amazing young man whose sense of humor I can promise you was above the level of a seven-year-old. He loved to laugh and was so much fun to be around.

At first, I remember being put off by Ronnie. In the beginning stages of living with this family, I was so nervous and somewhat queasy around the young man. All of his food had to be blended up for him and watching him be fed was a hard task to do simply because of the choking and spit up. It was not an enjoyable experience, to say the least. However, I found as my heart grew fonder of Ronnie the things that at first troubled me didn't bother me as much as in the beginning. When you start to truly care for someone, you are able to see past these things that would be deemed as gross, troubling, or off-putting.

I do recall one time in particular when I had to feed Ronnie to help out the host family I was living with. This was a true test for a young man with a weak stomach and good memory. The good memory means I would be able to recall memories and thus posses the ability to get sick all over again! Feeding Ronnie was brutal, to say the least. He was coughing, laughing, and spitting up. This was a culinary war zone. It's funny because I remember a point during this meal when I no longer was put off by the act of feeding him and instead started talking to him. He became calm and the rest of the meal went down with no problems. See, once I was able to speak to Ronnie out of care and love all things changed in me. It's really quite hilarious to think that Ronnie was probably thinking the whole time, "Sheesh, why can't this guy get it together and feed me right? This tattooed freak show isn't much for conversation!"

Over the months that I lived in this house I grew closer in friendship with Ronnie. Sometimes me and my friends Eric and Michelle, who were the children of this host family, would go to the mall with Ronnie and go to movies or just hang out. I learned through this process that loving someone means to do so with an open hand. This means to love someone regardless of what you get in return. Love is a forward motion and a spring of living water. Love is always giving and not interested in what can be given back. The entire world needs an open hand and that open hand is the Church.

One day we were getting Ronnie ready to go to the mall. I remember we were in the driveway with him. I forgot my jacket upstairs in the house so I quickly ran upstairs to get it. When I got to the second level of the home I stopped and paused to look out the big bay window that overlooks the cityscape. Then I began to look back into the yard and driveway where everyone was. I remember all of a sudden Ronnie's wheelchair started rolling forward ever so slightly. Then, in a breath, Ronnie and his wheelchair went rocketing down the hill. Ronnie's wheelchair hit the curb and Ronnie was thrown into a small quarry of jagged rocks next to a fence. This all happened within the span of 20 seconds, which seemed to go in slow motion.

I remember standing in the living room watching this all happen and not being able to move a muscle or do anything. I was completely frozen, knowing that there was absolutely nothing I could do to stop these events from taking place. The family rushed Ronnie inside and called 9-1-1. I heard Eric scream for me to come to the basement where they had just brought Ronnie to the bathroom. I walked down the stairs really afraid of what I might see. As I came around the corner I watched as they began to wash the blood off of Ronnie. I watched Ronnie's blood turn the water bright pink as he cried out. These scenes seemed to be a blur of frenzied activity, while maintaining the property of slow motion. It's something that only those who have dealt with trauma can understand or relate to.

When the ambulance workers came bursting through the door to get Ronnie I remember being in the moment for the first time. My eyes filled up with tears and I thought "God, please"…it was a simple, broken, heartfelt prayer from a prodigal for a friend he loved. They rushed Ronnie to the emergency room and we drove straight to the hospital to be with Ronnie. When we got there we waited for a long time in this off-white hallway with chairs, waiting until the doctor finally came out and said we could all come back to see Ronnie. We walked into the emergency room and went into Ronnie's room to see him sitting there smiling and happy to see us. Ronnie didn't have a single broken bone, only a few minor stitches and scrapes. I learned another valuable lesson that day…that love sometimes means having no control.

Chapter seven

Living Out of a New View

To see others through the filter of the Holy Spirit is possibly one of the hardest things for a believer to do. To allow the Holy Spirit to effect us so deeply in our perspectives is a power we cannot afford to not tap into. It is a very essential need for every believer to be able to live under the unction of the Holy Spirit. There is so much we just don't understand about ourselves and others. The Holy Spirit can bring that kind of revelatory understanding that is necessary to build the Kingdom of God in our lives and the lives of those around us. I believe that one of the greatest injustices we can commit against each other in community is the sin of familiarity. Something happens when you begin to know one another on a deeper level and you become friends. Often times, our relationships can be the proverbial apple in the garden. What I mean by that is that when we get to know someone we get to see who they are on a deeper level. At times, we can use that familiarity to dismiss the God in them. Just like in the Garden of Eden when Adam and Eve ate of the tree of knowledge they looked at one another without their Godly value and worth.

It is within human nature to measure those around us against ourselves. This can be due to either pride or low self-esteem, which happen to be two different heads of the same animal. Since we live in a fallen world, we must battle with the ungodly desires of our flesh. That word "flesh" is a tricky concept for us to understand. The flesh we struggle with is also the flesh that can become baptized by the power of the Holy Spirit to do great things. For example, your emotions can become a divisive beast that tears you down or brings utter destruction to others around you—based on what emotions you are allowing to control you. I have seen people destroy families through manipulation, willingly hurt others, and even put themselves at odds with the law. We desperately need to understand that our emotions can be our downfall or our strength.

In a lot of Christian circles people are very afraid to embrace their emotions, even to the point where they carry on throughout their lives being completely ignorant and numb. I have seen many hurting brothers and sisters in the Lord ignore and deny the reality of the pain that is in their hearts for fear that they will be exposed or viewed somehow as less Godly. These same ministers who are trying to live double lives hold down these deep feelings and continually surrender them to the enemy rather then allowing the Holy Spirit to come in and heal those emotions.

When it comes to your emotions, satan is in a desperate battle to keep you immature and locked up inside. The enemy would love nothing more than for you to ignore or keep your emotions locked up so at just the right time he can come along with a temptation and whisper it in your ear. He wants your suppressed emotions to boil over into sin. The Holy Spirit can take that pain, hiddenness, and heartache away from you and turn it into strength. Your emotions which you have allowed the enemy to use could be used for understanding, empathy, courage, and wisdom rather than confusion and self-love.

When I decided to write this specific book, I thought to myself, "This is going to have some very hands-on research." I was totally right to assume such a thing. Whenever the Lord wants to release strength to the Church, He brings those who have come through the Refiner's fire and have been tested pure. So, it's no surprise then that the Holy Spirit gave me a burden to view others through the filter of the Holy Spirit. This journey of getting doves eyes has been a remarkable one thus far and I am convinced it's not a journey that I will ever be done with here on earth.

We get this awesome responsibility when we become believers to live in community with other Christians. We are not enemies, but through Christ we are now a family. Ephesians Chapter 2 tells us Christ removed the walls of hostility that we use to keep each other separate. When we had that moment where we received salvation, whether at a church or at a ministry event or outreach, at that moment we gave up our own rights and inherited the rights of the Kingdom. See, when we were saved we were given peace, love, harmony, and dignity. This means each one of us was given these things. This means if it's a reality for me then it is a reality for my neighbor.

I remember a specific instance where the Holy

Spirit gave me an opportunity to walk out yet another facet of viewing others through transformed eyes. There was a young man I met and we will say, for the sake of privacy, his name is Rick. I never really knew Rick and, as a matter of fact, he never really knew me very well. Rick had shown up at a few events that I had spoken at and was a young, eager, and often overpowering young man. I remember getting frustrated with his constant attempts to contact me as well as his personal claims to greatness that he constantly spoke about. Yes, Rick had some issues with wanting to make connections for the sake of furthering his "Christian career," so to speak. It drives me crazy when people who either have pride or low self-esteem (which are closely related, contrary to what you might think) try to muscle their way into your life and ministry.

Rick was one of those individuals who really tested my leadership and relational skills, that's for sure. I found myself withdrawing even further from Rick. I was punishing Rick for his issues, you see...I was holding back relationship as a form of punishment so I could teach him a lesson without ever having to take on the responsibility of discipleship. It's interesting to look at it from that angle. It even stings a little that I would use a form of isolation to teach someone a lesson, someone who I wasn't even willing to take under my wing to really teach anything to. If you are a pastor or leader, please do not chastise those who you struggle with if you are not even willing to train them in the ways of Christ.

The Lord completely set me up for this character

development years before I met Rick. There was a time I found myself in a place that was very difficult in my life where I was walking out some healing. I was in such a fragile place and I had made some mistakes personally that put the Sheppard's rod over my character. I remember pacing and praying and recalling the fact that deep down inside I thought I was better than other people around me. These people who "got on my nerves" were viewed as less than me in my eyes. It's a brutal reality and not one I am proud of. When I was pacing and praying through this mess the Holy Spirit said, "Look around you," and I did. I saw all around me those people who I thought were worth less than myself. The Lord said, "They are better off than you." At that moment, I thought to myself, "Oh, how I wish I could become one of them rather than be in this situation. I would gladly switch places with this person than stay in this mess."

It wasn't until my circumstances were so broken that I realized how self-righteous I had really become. I took away the dignity of people around me and didn't see my own pride until my dignity had also been taken away. It is a humbling place to be when you see how little you have without Christ.

This led to many situations and opportunities where I could pour into the lives of some of the more "difficult" people around me. Yes, Rick and others just like him were lumped into this journey of humility and changing vision. I still remember the last interaction I had with Rick. He was going on about how he was a prophet and how powerful he was. All of a sudden, the Lord spoke to me and said, "Have mercy, son of David." I thought, "Well, that's strange." Then the Lord said, "I had mercy and you must have it as well." So, I began to pour myself out to Rick and to really teach him in a loving manner about the Kingdom. I received help from the Holy Spirit so I could look again through new eyes at Rick.

I remember when I let Rick in on the fact that I was frustrated with him. He stopped going on about himself and there was a moment of silence. Then Rick said, "I am sorry, but I have pride issues." At that moment, I was filled with even more understanding and compassion for Rick. I thought, "Oh Lord, he has been made aware and yet no leader in his life has ever made the time to teach him otherwise." I would like to tell you that this has been completely resolved and Rick and I are friends, but this is not the case. I am still on this journey with the Holy Spirit on loving and teaching. The good news is…we are getting there.

I think one of the most powerful things we can do as a community of believers is to keep everyone's dignity intact. When we walk according to the Spirit we will not gratify the desires of our flesh. This reality corresponds to how we think of others, what we say of others, and what we do to others as a result of our thoughts and speech. When we ask the Holy Spirit to give us His vision for others, then we are saying "yes" to an invitation to improve and deepen our own character. How will you ever love well if you don't attempt to love someone who isn't easy to love? To see people who we already love with kindness and affection does not stretch us. Even the enemies of God love those who love them. Nothing is added to us when we only love those who love us. When we allow our vision to be baptized with the Holy Spirit we get the strength and compassion of Christ Jesus to love others and allow them to keep their dignity.

There was a time when I lived in Kansas City that I very briefly worked with an inner healing ministry. I first went through a program that was designed to bring healing to those who are dealing with brokenness. It was a wonderful program that was confession and prayer based. After I went through the program one of the leaders asked me to join his team in Kansas City and consider working with a small men's group. I was excited at first about someone actually wanting to use me in some form of ministry. The reality is most young people in the western Church are not given much in the realm of leadership as they grow both in age and maturity. Too many kings and not enough thrones, you might say.

I remember that first night I came as a leader to the men's small group. I was excited about helping others. The reality was that I was being given an opportunity to get new vision from the Holy Spirit concerning the broken people around me. There was a group of about five men, ranging in age from 19 to 50 years old. We sat around at first, fought through the awkward silence, and eventually started making small talk about life and how things were currently going in each one of our lives. I thought to myself, "Well, this isn't so bad now is it? I can totally do this, no problem!"

However, when it came to confession time I was left disturbed, shocked, sick, and felt the need to go pray just to deal with what had been shared. I felt like I needed to go through a Holy Spirit hot shower to get the demonic issues off of me. Now, keep in mind all you who are reading this book, that at this time in my life I was learning and no longer hold to these views. I don't believe you "catch" what others are struggling with when you pray over them.

I found myself observing these men and thinking, "How could they do what they did?" I remember coming to the conclusion that these men would never live normal lives and, of course, some of them may not even make it into Heaven because of what they had done. However, I was very, very wrong and immature. This is why I was being taken on this journey with the Holy Spirit to see others as they are viewed by Heaven.

I decided to keep attending these meetings because even though it was more sobering than I had expected, there was also something inside me that wanted to see how God was going to deal with these men and these situations. During one of these sessions I remember a man confessed some darkness that he had come into agreement with. It shocked me and made me nervous and scared just to be near him. What happened next is what helped me to understand what the Lord felt about these men. The man, after confessing and repenting, fell onto his hands and started coughing. I thought, "Well, that's odd." Then the man vomited on the carpet. I never was shown this type of Christianity growing up! I had never heard of this kind of Jesus. The man looked up and his eyes were totally clear. His face had color for the first time since I had met him. He began to weep and thank Jesus. We prayed for this man and God totally delivered him that night.

Anytime I would see this same man, or really any of these men, I started to see the work and desire of God over them and in them. No longer was I disgusted or disturbed by the issues these men had. Instead I started getting Holy Spirit vision and thought we all have so much hope for our futures. Not just these men but also myself. We all hoped to become better men. I learned through this process the importance of not confusing people's struggles or weaknesses with who they really are in Christ Jesus.

The Holy Spirit has His own set of eyes that we can see through and the Holy Spirit has the ability to give us His hearing and speaking as well. This entire world can be changed if we walk according to the will of God in Jesus Christ and in the power of the Holy Spirit. If we can put on a new vision we can become powerful, loving, patient, kind, etc. We can become God's song to this world. We can become the answer to those who are asking, "Is God real and how can I know Him?" If you cannot see others and this world around you with the filter of the Holy Spirit then you will not be effective as an agent of love and change in this world.

We must also work to align our speech with our renewed vision. Our words can release life or death inside our heart as well as to others. Death and life are in the power of the tongue. (Prov. 18:21) Let your speech always be with grace, seasoned with salt, that you may know how you ought to answer each one. (Col. 4:6) Bless those who curse you...pray for those who spitefully use you. (Mt. 5:44) The most common way to grieve the Spirit is by our words. When the Spirit is grieved, He still loves us. However, we cannot receive from Him and participate with Him in the same measure.

There is so much that our language relates to in our lives. The book of James has some amazing things to say about how speech relates to our inner and outer lives. James 3:1-2 instructs, "My brethren, let not many of you become teachers, knowing that we shall receive a stricter judgment. For we all stumble in many things. If anyone does not stumble in word, he is a perfect man, able also to bridle the whole body." James teaches that if we focus on our speech we can control all our physical appetites. James gave us very helpful insights into overcoming addictions. Many do not focus enough on this. Most translate "perfect" as "mature." It is the same word used in James 1:4.

The teacher often focuses on getting the facts right, but James points out that their greatest challenge is their speech outside the classroom. James was pointing out the need for revelation to produce character change in the real world and in the heart. James uses three metaphors (the bit v. 3; rudder v. 4; small fire v. 5) to emphasize the truth that the tongue as a small member of our body is the key to controlling the much larger issues related to our body, life and relationships. James reveals the vast power of our tongues that is out of proportion to its size. Most frustration is an expression of our boasting in our greater insight. Indeed, we put bits in horses' mouths that they may obey us, and we turn their whole body. "Look also at ships: although they are so large and are driven by fierce winds, they are turned by a very small rudder wherever the pilot desires. Even so the tongue is a little member and boasts great things. See how great a forest a little fire kindles!" (James 3:3-5).

God requires humility that renounces grumbling and evil speaking against one another. "You be patient. Establish your hearts, for the coming of the Lord is at hand. Do not grumble against one another, brethren, lest you be condemned. Behold, the Judge is standing at the door!" (James 5:8-9) "Humble yourselves in the sight of the Lord, and He will lift you up. Do not speak evil of one another, brethren. He who speaks evil of a brother and judges his brother, speaks evil of the law and judges the law." (James 4:10-11)

There is power in our words and one of the greatest indicators of where you are at spiritually is your language because what goes on in the heart comes out our mouth. We know this from scripture (Mark 7:21). So to live out of a new view we must begin speaking well of others and doing our best to outdo one another in showing honor (Romans 12:10). We must represent ourselves in truth and not just use meaningless words but back up our words with loving action.

Chapter eight

Becoming Motivated by Love

I sat in a meeting once at a ministry I served at for a number of years. We were discussing the purpose of rewards pertaining to Heaven and our time and service here on earth. An enthusiastic young man began to share a story about how much he loved going out to feed the homeless or bless others. He went on to share that the reason he did this and kept it secret was due to the idea that every time he served it would add wealth to his home in Heaven. I sat there totally shocked at this idea that was introduced in this leadership meeting. I spoke up and said if love is not our primary motivation, then serving others doesn't count as a Christian act. It takes nothing to serve from the place of the promise of monetary compensations, either here on earth or in Heaven.

Love must be the compass from which we are guided into serving others. In this meeting I was labeled as an idealist because of my belief in love being our primary motivation. The senior leader said we, as humans, are selfish by nature and the idea of rewards is all that will truly motivate us. If we serve at all as humans, it's because we receive. I personally do not believe this type of broken theology and belief system. I think that once we are filled with the Holy Spirit we can serve from the place of love and not from a selfish place. Love is an open hand and an outgoing flowing motion that does not seek selfish desires. That is the very nature of God, because God is love and God is motivated by love due to the fact that He is love.

This is how I think about being motivated by love. Let's say a young man meets a young lady and she is everything he ever wanted in another person. He asks her out on a date and she says, "Well, it is socially acceptable that I accept this request, so I believe I will go with you on a date." Don't you think he might feel like perhaps he no longer wants to go on a date with this young lady? Or let's say for another example you have a spouse and you are discussing your heartfelt desire to keep the house in one place and out of complete disarray. Your spouse says, "Well, I am married to you so I will clean up the house because that is what is expected of me." Now how would that feel? Some of you wives may just say, "Well, that works for me!" Ha-ha. But the truth is that you want someone to do things for you or with you based on the fact that they love you and not just because it's what's expected of them. Obligation is not the same thing as choosing to serve out of love.

The Lord is right now moving the Church into a place of authentic devotion and love. For too long the Church has lived out of this place of obligation to the Lord rather than real relationship with Him as a Father and King. So many people are even right now sitting in church pews totally numb on the inside as it relates to the Lord and the love that He has made available to us. We have become those who stumble around in the dark trying to grasp out for any sign of salvation and love. The truth is that Jesus is present in our lives. He is not an absentee landlord, but rather a God who is deeply involved in our lives and hearts. We can run around confusing being busy with having real relationship when the truth is at times we are just busy and completely void of real relationships. I know many people from my time working in the corporate world who are far too busy and their families suffer. Some people are convinced they are giving their children a better future, but at the same time they are robbing them of a mother or father—thus causing major identity issues and destiny confusion. This type of living has broken hearts for years and caused many to have hearts of stone rather than hearts of flesh.

A great example of this topic is the story of Hosea and Gomer. Hosea was a prophet and a faithful man of God. Gomer was a prostitute who Hosea fell in love with and God told Hosea to make her his wife. How would you respond today if you knew a faithful pastor who felt the Lord was telling him to rescue a prostitute and marry her? This is something that was considered taboo and I am sure the religious community of Hosea's day had a lot to say about this union and the kind of man Hosea was. Hosea and his prostitute of a wife became a literal "talk of the town" in his day. And yet this is a poignant picture of the kind of love that we are talking about in this chapter. The kind of choosing to love that makes a public mockery of darkness.

Hosea arrived on the scene during a dark time in Israel's history where they were struggling with apostasy. The Lord used Hosea to give some powerful messages to call a nation out of an adulterous relationship with other gods. God is a jealous God and used Hosea to illustrate this kind of love and jealousy. This is the perfect picture of how we can get trapped into harlotry relating to our relationship with God. Hosea came and married a loose woman who had a really bad reputation. She was a known prostitute in the city that Hosea called home. The reason this was such an awesome example of love is because Gomer was undeserving and unfaithful. Yet, Hosea was able to show her mercy and reconciliation when she didn't deserve it.

Hosea is such a powerful book relating to the power of love. After Gomer had cheated on Hosea several times (it is believed historically that she had children with other men) still the Lord God told Hosea, "Go back to her and show her your love." Which means go love on her Hosea and let everyone in town see you buy her back. When Hosea's heart was broken and he turned to the Lord with his sorrow the Lord caused Hosea's heart to turn back to Gomer for the purpose of walking out a picture of what God does with us. See we are Gomer and God is like Hosea in our story. Now Hosea could have simply just said, "Yes Lord, because I serve you and you are bigger than me I will go and do what you say." But instead Hosea allowed the Lord to give him the ability to keep finding it in his own heart and will to love her.

In the story of Hosea, God was showing the people of Israel how He felt about them and what they had done in relationship with their God. There are many lessons to be learned from the story of Hosea that we can implement in our own lives. One of the main draws of the story of Hosea and Gomer is that she was a prostitute and he was a man of God, a prophet of God. We see in looking at this story how we can be like Gomer in relationship to God. We often play the harlot and forsake our first love because we don't understand what healthy, trusting, and loving relationships look like or feel like. Most of our intimacy is broken and we struggle to trust those we hold closest to our hearts. It is no wonder that we struggle with choosing love...love requires us to drop our defenses.

One of the beautiful things about the story and life of Hosea and Gomer is the grace factor. We get to understand the view of others through the filter of grace. This can be really difficult for us to understand and operate in simply because of our issues in this life. We struggle to view others through grace and love because we treat grace as a precious commodity that must be protected outside of ourselves. Grace is a free gift to all through Jesus Christ. When we give ourselves grace for our issues and hang-ups we find comfort and sometimes apathy. But when it comes to assisting in delegating that grace to others (and that's really all we are doing is assisting), we freak out and struggle to show the same level of love and grace we ourselves can take advantage of. We believe that grace makes us special and if we extend that grace to someone else then that will make them special. When everyone is special to God, then we think that no one is. We can quickly get under the impression that we all can't be equal in God's eyes and thus we withhold from others the very thing we are not stewarding rightly. You see,

Gomer didn't get what she deserved and neither do we. Amen.

As time has gone on, I am learning more about myself and others relating to ministry and the work of the Kingdom of God. I remember when I first started ministering I thought, "Man, this is amazing and I hope I can make it big someday and speak at all the major conferences. Wow, wouldn't that be amazing?" My young heart had the wrong motivation for ministry. This is something the Lord has spent the last decade working out of me. I have lost my desire to be great so I can sell teachings or books, but rather my eyes have been opened to the truth of all those things. It is amazing when the Lord promotes you. The only real way to be promoted in the Kingdom of God is through God Himself. But things can get funny when you don't know why you are supposed to do what you do. God is willing to show you why you are called to minister if you are willing to listen.

There was one time my wife and I were asked to come minister in a small town which will remain unnamed. I was very excited about the opportunity and had great expectations (delusion and pride) concerning this conference. The Lord had given me this awesome prophetic word for the Church and the entire city. I could hardly wait to go and deliver the word. I spent time praying and getting myself ready for this event. The day we were leaving I could hardly sit still because I had all these ideas of the great things I would do while I was there. Don't get me wrong, I was not completely prideful, I know to a degree the measure of the man I am. To be totally honest, most people in my life would have had no idea I felt this way or thought this way, but in my heart I knew this was an area of pride.

We arrived in the city and I met the pastor and his wife at the hotel they had booked for us. The hotel was small and dirty, so needless to say I was not really excited about staying at this particular spot. I thought, "Oh well, Lord thank you anyways for this room." Then the pastor and his wife took us out to eat and it was what some might refer to as a dive. I was actually a little nervous to eat the food (kind of like a Pharisee). They then dropped off my wife and I at the hotel for the night and I voiced my reservations about coming to minister at this church. My wife Grace is exactly her namesake; she is full of wisdom, prophetic insight, integrity, and grace. She told me that maybe I just needed to be thankful for what the Lord was doing with us. Oh boy was she right! I have learned so much from my wife in relation to character. The Lord has used her to help make me a better husband, minister, and all around better person. So, after this conversation we went to sleep ready for the next day.

I woke up in the morning and I thanked God for whatever He was doing with this event. I told Him I just wanted to be used by Him and gave Him permission to do a work in my heart and character relating to these kinds of issues. I really did feel peace from the Lord about my perspective at this point and I felt ready to bring the Word of the Lord at this event. The pastors picked us up at the hotel and we drove to the church for the first time since we had been in town. As we pulled up to the church I looked and saw this rundown little building. That was not being critical, it was really rundown and dilapidated by most people's standards.

As we walked up the staircase to the one room building, I started to feel the Holy Spirit tug on my heart for these people and this area. I asked the Holy Spirit to please help me see how He sees and for the strength to please God in the entire ministry I do for Him. We walked into the building and there was this small church with around 14 people in little metal chairs waiting for the speaker to arrive. I had my assistant with me and we were setting up our resource table, which was hilarious considering the amount of people there and the neighborhood we were in. The Lord was showing me how worthless my self-effort was.

Looking at this small group of people, I thought, "Lord, help me." They started worship and they had no worship team, only a tape player with two singers leading worship. I spoke to the Lord and said, "Give me eyes to see what You are saying here." At that very moment, I heard the Holy Spirit say, "It can never be about the money or your reputation." After hearing this I sat next to Grace and said, "Honey, I am sorry for the way I have viewed this trip." I began to tell her what the Lord was saying to me about faith and motives. She agreed wholeheartedly and we prayed together in our little metal folding chairs and told God we would not make it about the money.

I was introduced and the Lord moved mightily in that service that morning. There were words of knowledge, prophetic words, and salvations that took place. The prophetic word for the city and church was later confirmed to us after speaking it. And at the end of this event a sweet little old woman walked up to my wife and me and said she had a word to share with us. This woman was their prophet and she had a heart of gold, to say the least. We began praying and she said that she had been asked by the pastor to pray for us and she was so nervous because she thought, "Lord, what can I do?" She said she felt silly even giving the word she had received from the Lord. I told her you have to give it if it's from God because He knows what's best in relation to what we need. So, she said she watched us walk into the church and heard the Lord say, "I want you to tell them I said 'thank you.'" Of course by this time my wife and I were in tears because we understood what she was releasing. It wasn't just that the Lord was saying thank you for coming to this small church and giving your all. He was saying something even bigger than that to us that day and it was thank you for saying yes to my invitation of humility and having the right heart motives.

God loves it when we become motivated by love rather than economy or a desire to be great for our own name's sake. I saw those people at that church with the love of the Holy Spirit and that became the reason I ministered the way I did. I didn't minister well so that I could take up a large offering or be looked at as a powerful man of God, but rather my heart was motivated to see the people ministered to and set free. That is love, that is Jesus…and that is the whole point.

In the years I have spent as a counselor I have met many people who have different motivations for why they do what they do. Some people perform so that they will be accepted and hopefully that acceptance will grow into love. Others don't make any effort at all because of their wounds and self-defeating thoughts. The one thing I have noticed about all the people I have counseled is that they want love and they want to be viewed with the eyes of love. Some of the most selfish, deceived, and broken people I have met at the very core of who they are just really want to be loved by God and others. This is a God design.

No matter what culture you're in people have basic needs. This is something that transcends people groups and geography. People everywhere have a basic core need for love. People want to be known as they really are. I have met so many ministers with double lives who are scared out of their minds to be seen for who they are. Many of the reasons they are in that broken place are because they were afraid in the first place to be known due to rejection. Most of us want to be known, but through the things we suffer in this life we become hidden.

To see one another with the eyes of love is to ask how Jesus views people. Jesus is so full of compassion and He executes that compassion with excellence. Jesus loves others perfectly and never once fails in anything He sets out to do. The beautiful thing is that through Jesus we can view others through that same filter of the Holy Spirit. Jesus had perfect obedience when it came to functioning in this life and we get to step into that perfection when we choose Christ.

We have this understanding of the perfection of Jesus and we look at our own failures and weakness, rather than seeing our failures and weakness eclipsed by His perfection made available to us through His death and resurrection. Everything Jesus did He made available to us so we could spread the Kingdom.

The two most important commandments in the Bible have to do with our ability to see ourselves and others through the filter of the Holy Spirit. "Teacher, which is the great commandment in the law? Jesus said, "'You shall love the Lord your God with all your heart, with all your soul, and with all your mind.' This is the first and great commandment. The second is like it: 'You shall love your neighbor as yourself.' On these two commandments hang all the Law and the Prophets." (Matthew 22:36-40)

The foundational premise of this is that people who love Jesus will love others much more. It is impossible to love Jesus and not love people more. The greatest anointing of the Spirit is to walk in the two great commandments by loving Jesus with all our heart and our neighbor as ourselves. To put the second commandment first is to make our ministry an idol in our heart. Jesus answered the question about which was the great commandment by quoting Deuteronomy 6:5: "You shall love the Lord your God with all your heart."

He added three new ideas. First, that loving God is the first and greatest thing. Second, that loving people is like loving God. Third, the purpose of God as seen in Scripture hangs on, or originates from, these commandments.

Chapter nine

The Four Stages of Love

I learned some powerful things during the time I served at the House of Prayer in Kansas City. Mike Bickle taught some amazing things which he has given me permission to use. Mike spoke about the four stages of love and I believe, from a counselor's perspective, that they are right on the money pertaining to the stages or phases of basic love.

Stage #1: receiving revelation of God's love for us (Eph. 3:18-19). Knowing how God feels about us as our Father and Bridegroom as the foundational truth that equips us to love God. "We love Him because He first loved us." (1 Jn. 4:19)

Stage #2: receiving God's love for Jesus. It takes God's power to love God. "I [Jesus] have declared to them Your [the Father] name ... that the love with which you loved Me may be in them." (Jn. 17:26) "The love of God has been poured out in our hearts by the Holy Spirit." (Rom. 5:5)

Stage #3: loving ourselves in the grace of God. We love our neighbor as we love ourselves in the grace of God by knowing who we are in Christ (2 Cor. 5:17), along with rejoicing in who God made us (personality, gifting, calling, physical features, etc; Ps. 139:13-17). Agreeing with God about our value is different from loving ourselves in a selfish way. As we get our eyes off of others (envy) and off our failures (condemnation), we value and even love who God made us.

Stage #4: loving others is the greatest work of the Spirit and is the ultimate proof of His work in the human heart. As we love God and ourselves, we overflow in love for others. It is the visible measurement of our invisible love for God. "That you love one another...By this all will know that you are My disciples." (Jn. 13:34-35) "Let us not love in word or in tongue, but in deed and in truth. And by this we know that we are of the truth, and shall assure our hearts before Him." (1 Jn. 3:18-19)

To love our neighbor is to show love to Christ Jesus on this earth. Often when we take the time to show kindness to those around us we are ministering to Jesus as well as acting as His ambassadors. It is kind of a two way street when you think about it. We serve Him in two ways when we stop for a moment to see Jesus in others and ourselves. "The second is like it: 'You shall love your neighbor as yourself.'" (Mt. 22:39) First, love for others, like loving God, flows from regularly encountering God's love for us. "We love Him because He first loved us." (1 Jn. 4:19) Second, to walk in genuine love as defined by God is much more than sentimentalism. It takes seeking to love Jesus with "all" our heart, mind, soul, and strength. Third, to walk in love requires the Spirit's power to energize us; we regularly need our emotions stirred and strengthened by the subtle impressions of the Spirit. Christianity is an ongoing encounter of love with a Person. "The love of God has been poured out in our hearts by the Holy Spirit." (Rom. 5:5)

Only by loving Jesus and ourselves are we able to consistently overflow in love for others. We are energized to sustain compassion by the gratitude and joy of being loved by God. We must love God first, and then love ourselves, to properly love our neighbor. We must love ourselves first to have power and energy to love others. We can only love our neighbor in the overflow of loving God, for only in being loved by God and in loving God can we properly love others. This demanding commandment requires a comprehensive re-ordering of how we think and process life. We by nature are self-consumed, so it takes the power of the Spirit to walk this out.

Loving God and loving ourselves are bound up as one. We value others in the overflow of seeing how valuable God is and how valuable we are to God. The second commandment seems to stand by itself in some passages because its connection to the first commandment is assumed. We are not called to love others "instead of" ourselves but "as" ourselves—by using the same standard in measuring love for others as we use for ourselves. We are to seek our neighbors' benefit "as," or with the same focus and energy, as we seek our own benefit. For example, we are to seek for more money and blessing so we can give more. In this God's generosity is manifest to us and through us.

To love others as ourselves is to value their longing for significance, acceptance, and success as being as important as our own. Because all people are created in God's image, they deserve to receive love from us (the love that we receive from God). We are not to dismiss loving ourselves, but we enhance it by loving others with new depth. We will experience God's tender compassion as we show it to others. This radical command touches the core of our being. This command exposes a deep root system of sin in us. To seek to love people as ourselves shows us our sin and spiritual lack. When we focus on loving and serving others it is a stark contrast to the inward focus that most of us call home. Just like how fasting brings to the surface what controls you so does loving your neighbor as yourself.

By saying, "On these two commandments hang the Law and Prophets" (Mt. 22:40), Jesus emphasizes their importance and how connected they are to each other and God's eternal purposes. God's purposes as declared in the Law and Prophets depend, or hang (like a bucket on a rope), on love. Love is the source behind all of God's eternal purposes. Our love for God and the goal of the Scripture are fulfilled when we love others. Love is the practical expression of what the teachings in the Law and the Prophets really mean. "He who loves another has fulfilled the law. The commandments, "You shall not commit adultery," "You shall not murder," "You shall not steal,"...are summed up in this saying, "You shall love your neighbor as yourself."...Love is the fulfillment of the law." (Rom. 13:8-10) Paul gives us more insight into love by exhorting us to offer it as from a pure heart (our motive to enrich others without seeking for personal benefit), from a good conscience that is free from condemnation (Rom. 8:1), and from sincere faith that stands steady in difficult circumstances. "The purpose ["goal," NIV] of the commandment is love from a pure heart, from a good conscience, and from sincere faith." (1 Tim. 1:5)

Love is both the goal (Mt. 7:12; Rom. 13:8-10) and source of the Law and Prophets. In other words, all of God's purposes in the Scripture hang on these two great commandments. We must understand the Golden Rule in its context in the Sermon on the Mount, which calls us to an all-consuming relationship with God. In this passage, Jesus taught us the Father gives good things to those who ask in prayer. Next, He said, "Therefore, whatever you want men to do to you, do also to them." In other words, this commandment is given in context to the call to prayer. "Ask, and it will be given to you; seek, and you will find...Everyone who asks receives...Or what man is there among you who, if his son asks for bread, will give him a stone?...How much more will your Father...give good things to those who ask! Therefore, whatever you want men to do to you, do also to them, for this is the Law and the Prophets." (Mt 7:7-12)

The call to walk in love is given in context of God releasing His supernatural provision to us by prayer. The foundation of this commandment is a revelation of the Father's love and a prayer life based on trusting His leadership. An important aspect of loving people is seen in embracing a lifestyle of fasting and prayer so that we are prepared to release more of the power of the Spirit to everyone around us. The lives of John the

Baptist, Elijah, Paul, and the apostles testify to this. Love is rightly focused on meeting people's physical needs with food and clothing. However, since people are eternal spiritual beings, they need more than having their physical needs meet. Love requires more than sentimental humanism, which lacks a relationship to Jesus on God's terms. Allegiance to Jesus provides us the standard and source to be properly motivated and energized in love.

One core issue at the end of the age will be in how love is defined. We must define love on God's terms, not by the humanistic culture that seeks love without reference to obedience to Jesus. The true definition of love and good works is found in allegiance to Jesus. Love draws people to truth (not to us), providing opportunity for their greater eternal need to be met in Jesus. Secular humanism is content to help people without meeting their deeper spiritual need. We love God as we seek to enrich others on Jesus' terms.

The supreme value of love can only be understood when it is set in context to the eternal realm of the Judgment Seat of Christ (Rom. 14:10-12; 2 Cor. 5:10). Paul emphasized that all believers will give an account of their life and ministry to God (1 Cor. 3:10-15). "Though I speak with the tongues of men and of angels, but have not love, I have become sounding brass or a clanging cymbal. Though I have the gift of prophecy, and understand all mysteries...but have not love, I am nothing. Though I bestow all my goods to feed the poor, and...Give my body to be burned, but have not love, it profits me nothing." (1 Cor. 13:1-3). Paul gives us the essence of love as suffering long (by not judging harshly) and in being kind (v. 4a). Paul defines how love does not act by using eight negatives (vv. 4b-6b) and how it does act in using five positives (vv. 6-7). "Love suffers long and is kind; love does not envy; love does not parade itself, is not puffed up; does not behave rudely, does not seek its own, is not provoked, thinks no evil; does not rejoice in iniquity, but rejoices in the truth; bears all things, believes all things, hopes all things, endures all things." (1 Cor. 13:4-7) The superiority of love is seen in its permanence in eternity. "Love never fails. But whether there are prophecies, they will fail [pass away]." (1 Cor. 13:8)

Love never fails because every movement of our heart in love is remembered and rewarded by God forever at the Judgment Seat of Christ, whether it is received by people or not. No investment of love is forgotten, wasted or lost in God's sight. "God is not unjust to forget your work and labor of love which you have shown toward His name, in that you have ministered to the saints, and do minister." (Heb. 6:10) Love is the greatest. Faith (agreement with God's Word) is the way to release the gifts of the Spirit. Love is the purpose for them. Faith is how the gifts function. Love is why they function. Hope stabilizes us. We must be strong in faith and anchored in hope to walk in love. "Now abide faith, hope, love ... the greatest of these is love." (1 Cor. 13:13)

Chapter ten

Where Jesus Finds His Identity

Jesus is the premier example of loving God with all His soul and with a right identity, with a kingdom identity. Now, none of us have that identity by nature. We focus on it and we cultivate it. We have to sign up for it thousands of times, and we lose our way and sign up again. Jesus' identity is rooted in the fact that He loves God the Father and He loves people. That is where His identity is. It is in love. His identity is in His humility. Jesus' identity is not in the response people gave Him when He was here on the earth. The place where Jesus' humility is most clearly expressed is when He became a man and died on the cross. Let's read Philippians 2:6-8: "Jesus, who being in the form of God…" (v. 6, paraphrased). This is Paul talking. There is some really unusual language here if you are not familiar with these three verses, but these three verses are a goldmine. They are an absolute goldmine of truth. This is a steak that you could eat for ten years! If you studied only these three verses for years you would never exhaust them. They are so vast in their meaning.

"Jesus, being in the form of God…" (v. 6, paraphrased). So, He had the form of God. He had all the power of God. He had all the privileges that go with having all the power of God. That is what it means to be in the form of God. He had all the power and He had all the privileges that go with the power. It was all His. He was in the form of God. "He did not consider it robbery"—that is an interesting phrase—"to be equal with God, but He made Himself of no reputation" (v. 6–7). A number of translations say, "He emptied Himself." Jesus emptied Himself or He emptied Himself of reputation. That is what this is talking about. He decided He would live in a way without any regard to how the people responded to Him or gave Him recognition or affirmation. He emptied Himself of living for human affirmation. That is one part of this, it is bigger than that, but it is a part of it.

"Taking the form of a bondservant" (v. 7). Now, He took on the form of a bondservant. He adopted the outward lifestyle of a bondservant. It means that when people saw Him through His words and actions, He exhibited the behavior of a servant. The reason He took on the form of a bondservant when He became a man, is because for all eternity He had a servant's heart. Jesus did not become a servant when He became a man. He always had a servant's heart, but when He became a man His servant heart was openly seen in the human arena.
In the ancient world and even in our world today, being a servant was not something that was esteemed. It was actually a real put-down because the word means a slave. A man in the ancient world, who was a slave, had very little value. That is how He exhibited His behavior, like a slave, and nobody knew the truth about who He was. The reason He took on the form or the outward behavior of a slave is because inwardly He had a servant's heart.

It says that He became of no reputation. He decided when He was in the human arena that He would not live in regard to how men valued Him. He made Himself of no reputation. He said in effect, "I am not going to live by what they say about Me. If they completely ignore Me, I am going to live the same way before God. If they want to make Me king, I will not be king except by the will of God. I will not go high. I will go low. I will be of no reputation. What they say will not move Me in any way." This is remarkable. "And He came in the likeness of a man, being found in the appearance of a man" (Phil. 2:7–8, paraphrased). Now, that seems pretty cool. Being human is really awesome unless you are the uncreated God. Then, being human is a real step down. For the rest of creation, being human is a step up, but for the uncreated God to be human was a dynamic, significant limitation and restraint. This is a huge statement.

When He became man—the incarnation, when He was born—I cannot imagine what the angels said. I cannot wait to talk to them face-to-face on a regular basis and ask them things like, "What did you think when Jesus became human?" They may say, "Oh my goodness, it shocked all of us. We could hardly even believe the report." Maybe they will say it all differently. It is shocking. There is nothing to compare it to. Even a king in a palace becoming a slave in the field does not compare to God becoming human.

Let's look at this strange phrase: "Jesus did not consider it robbery to be equal with God" (v. 6). So, to be equal with God means to be equal in privilege and in honor, to be equal in the privileges that are God's. You can apply this two different ways. I believe both ways are valid. Both ways have an application. Jesus could have said that He would not take anything from God the Father by insisting on having the equal privileges that God the Father enjoyed, because He is as much God as the Father. But that would not have been robbery.

Then, on the other side of the spectrum, He did not consider it robbery—or take anything from Himself—if He refused all the privileges. Here He is—God—but refusing all the privileges. He can take them all and He would not be stealing anything from the Father or He can refuse them all and would not be stealing anything from His identity or the glory of who He is. He could have gone in either direction. He could have said, "I want all the privileges of the Father." The Father would not have looked over the balcony of Heaven and said, "Hey, wait, you are taking all of My privileges," because Jesus deserves the Father's privileges. It would not have been robbery.

Now, the angels might have looked at Him and said, "How come You are living like a poor man? You are God." Jesus might have said, "It does not take anything for Me to live like this, because My identity is not in what I have before men. My identity is in My relationship with the Father. My identity is in humility and in love, not in what I get from men during My thirty-three years on the earth." You have to read these notes a bit and say, "Huh, intense. What did I just read? I don't know, but it was intense." That is OK, but what I am saying is to take these notes and a few of the phrases and just work on them. Take them to the Lord in prayer and say, "Lord, write this on my heart."

After the incarnation, after Jesus became human, He had two natures. He was fully God and fully man. Now, the Father only has one nature. Jesus is the only one in existence who has two natures. No human has two natures and the Father and the Spirit only have one nature, but Jesus has two: He is fully God and fully man.

This is a great mystery. Though He was never less than God for the thirty-three years that He was on the earth, He lived as though He was never more than a man, meaning, He had the form of God, and He had the power to greatly influence people. In the form of God, He had all the power of God and all the rights to use it. That is what it means to have the form of God. He had all the power and all the rights to use it to influence people, but it was as if He said, "No, I am not going to do it. I am going to be like every other godly person. I am going to pray, fast, and wait on the Spirit, and when the Spirit leads Me, then I will use God's power to influence people. I will wait on the Spirit like every other human being has to."

Now, it was essential that Jesus took on this humility because if He was going to qualify as a human savior, a human high priest, He had to live totally within the boundaries of humanity. So, you could interview Jesus and say, "Jesus, how are You doing with this significant downgrade of being human? How are You handling this? Is it really hard to get used to?" Jesus might say, "The humility is necessary," because He had to live within these restraints in order to qualify as a human savior for us. He might say, "It does not make any difference to Me. My humility has been in place from eternity past. I do not get My identity from My power before people. My identity is in humility and in love. It is not in what people do. It is not in how they respond to Me.

In denying Himself of these privileges by being a servant, Jesus did not deny His true identity, but rather He was actually being true to Himself. When He was a servant it was not an exterior role. He did not take on a foreign role or put on a foreign garment. When He was a servant He was totally at home and He was true to His true self, because He has been a servant from eternity past.
When He is the king of the earth in the Millennial Kingdom, when He will be openly seen as King, He will be one hundred percent a servant. He will be the same.

Isaiah 53:2–3 is an interesting passage. "He has no form or comeliness, and when we see Him, there is no beauty that we should desire Him. He is despised and rejected...and we did not esteem Him." Jesus emptied Himself of His reputation in the eyes of men, because as a man He embraced this lifestyle of a servant. He had to do it in order to enhance us, because He could not have saved us if He did not live in the constraints of humanity. He had to be human to do it. He had to keep the rules, so to speak, and stay inside the boundary lines of humanity if He was going to be a human savior. That was no problem for Him because His core identity is humility and love.

So, as He embraced this lifestyle, every single person who met him, every person without exception—His mother, His father, everyone—greatly underestimated Him and they underestimated His abilities. When He was twenty years old, living in the neighborhood, not one human being had any idea how superior His intellect and abilities were. He had no need to show them in order to garner a response which would enhance His life to make it better. It was as if He said, "I have no need to show how unique and how superior I am." The opposite is true of us. We get our identity by recognition from people. We go out of our way to show how unique and superior we are. We work overtime to prove we have more than everybody else has. Here is Jesus, twenty years old, walking through town, far more intelligent, far more powerful, far more gifted than His closest companions ever knew. Even the twelve apostles never knew.

When Jesus visits John on the island of Patmos sixty or seventy years later, John, who knew Jesus best, fell like a dead man. He looked at Jesus and said, "Aaaghh!" Jesus might have said to him, "You did not really know Me that well, did you?" It is as if John said, "I had no idea You were at this level." Jesus might have said, "I am way beyond this." But think about it: nobody knew how superior He was. Nobody knew how distinct He was. He appeared ordinary with no special form. That meant He had no status in society. If you saw Him in a crowd there is nothing about His physical appearance that would cause you to pick Him out of the crowd. He had no specific attraction that made people turn their heads and notice Him. He was completely at peace in His spirit and completely at peace in His heart. Now, that is an identity based in God. He is our example.

What was most important to Jesus was to tell the Father's story, to make the Father known and to redeem our lives by dying for us. He was absolutely preoccupied in making the Father known and enriching our lives. What kind of applause did Jesus get? Even His main guys denied Him and at His resurrection, when Mary Magdalene said He rose from the dead, they did not even believe her. They said in effect, "No way, He did not rise." His main guys did not buy it.

If His core identity was in having power over people, then the incarnation would have been a denial of His true self. The reason I say this statement is because He existed not for man but rather for His own rule and reign. When He became a man, He did not deny His true self. His identity is in love and humility, not in showing His power. He showed His power in order to accomplish the will of God, but it did not enhance who He is. I am just guessing, but when I think about Jesus, I do not think that when Jesus walked around the earth

He said, "Oh, boy, do I have power!" I mean, He did Genesis 1.

I believe when He walked around the earth He thought, "Oh, how I love to love." It is as if you meet a little baby, an infant, and you get right up next to him and say, "OK, little guy, let's arm wrestle right now, you and me. Come on, put it right there." And he cannot even put his arm up. Then you say, "OK, forget the arm wrestling. I want to show you my superior power. Bring the chess board out right now. I am going to set you in your place." The little guy would look up and just spit. When an adult sees a little baby, they do not say, "Wow, do I have power over you!" An adult sees a little baby and says, "Wow, I love you."

When Jesus was among His people, He was not thinking about how to wow them. He was thinking about how He loved them. He had so much more power that it was not even an issue. People were always trying to get Him to prove His power. It was as if He was saying, "That is like arm wrestling a baby. I do not need to show Myself superior. There is no point in it." It is like playing chess with a baby. When you see a baby, you do not think, "Wow, do I have power over you." You think, "Wow, I love you. Wow, I feel for you. I want to make your life strong." Jesus' identity is not in His power. His identity is in His love. That is where He lives.

Jesus does not serve to prove something, but when He serves He expresses the truth of who He is. He was so comfortable washing the feet of the disciples.

There was nothing un-God like about washing feet. He was true to Himself. He had that same heart a billion years ago and He will have it a billion years from now. He will always love washing feet. This is what He is like, because His identity is in the right place. The Lord says to us, "Love Me with all your soul. Establish your identity in your relationship with Me and you will love Me with so much more clarity and depth."

Chapter eleven

The Father's Heart

Jesus came to reveal the Father to the human race and to offer relationship with Him. Jesus came to earth to be an offering for our sin and to reveal the personality of the Father to the human race. He came to reveal the Father in a Jewish context, which saw God as the transcendent creator as seen in Genesis 1. The Jews kept their distance and trembled before this God. Jesus taught that God was a Father. He has the affections, commitments and desire for a close personal relationship like a father. The Jews and Gentiles were to draw near with confidence before this kind, tenderhearted God. If we understood Jesus' teaching, mission and personality, then we would know the Father. To read the Gospels and interpret them accurately is to know the Genesis 1 God as our Father. As we study the Gospels to see what Jesus said and did, we learn about the personality of the Father.

Jesus' personality, ministry and teachings were profoundly attractive to the disciples. They so enjoyed being in His presence. He taught that if they knew the Father, they would see the same attractiveness in His personality. They would tremble before God's great power as creator, but would also have confidence in God's presence because of His great affections as a Father.

God's names reveal different facets of His personality. He has over 300 names in Scripture. The fatherhood of God dominated Jesus' teaching about God. From the beginning, God had a Father's heart and wanted a family to share His love with in deep relationship. Jesus emphasized the affectionate, deeply involved, relational dimension of God's personality as a Father. The Holy Spirit reaches to God through us as the "Spirit of adoption" crying, "Abba." Abba is a term of endearment like "Papa." It is respectful, yet affectionate and intimate.

The Spirit of adoption is the person of the Holy Spirit. He is also called the Spirit of comfort, truth, hope, holiness, conviction, power, etc. These various names of the Holy Spirit give us insight into how He ministers to us as believers. As the Spirit of adoption, He reveals the glory of our position as adopted sons and daughters. He convinces us of the truths or benefits related to being adopted by God. Being adopted speaks of a legal position of privilege in which the child became an heir of the family name, resources and estate. By our new position as adopted children we have access to the Father's heart in a unique way. The Spirit convinces us that we can encounter God's heart as our Abba. The "Abba revelation" empowers us to endure difficulty and to reject Satan's accusations that we are hopeless failures.

The measure of the Father's love for Jesus is the measure of His love for us. This is the ultimate revelation of our worth. It gives every believer the right to view themselves as "God's favorite." The Father feels about you in the same way that He feels about Jesus. He will not increase in His love for Jesus nor will He ever love anyone more than He loves Jesus. Therefore, since He loves you in the same way, He will never increase or decrease in the measure He loves you. Ask the Holy Spirit to guide you into the truth about the Father loving you like He loves Jesus. (John 16:13) Our lives are broken and unsettled without a "stabilizing anchor" until we know the embrace of the Father as our Abba. We need the assurance that we are enjoyed by God in our weakness.

I remember a time when I was growing in my understanding of the prophetic and prophetic ministry and God gave me an awesome invitation. I remember I was hearing so clearly and I would search out scripture to get messages from the Fathers Heart. I would worship and ask God to give me revelation concerning prophetic words. I would pray for a greater gifting of prophecy all the time when I was starting out. Desiring to prophecy is a great thing and biblical, however I was relating to God out of my gifting and calling rather than desiring to get near to His Heart. One day the Lord gave me a strong prophetic word for an individual and I couldn't wait to give it and then the Lord stopped me on my way to give the word. I asked Him "why don't you want me to say this prophetic word?" and the Lord said "I told you because you are my friend not so you could go share this word". That one statement showed me what my motives were and thank God I matured into something greater, which is the motive of love.

God does not confuse spiritual immaturity with rebellion. God loves unbelievers, yet He loves and enjoys believers. He immediately rejoices over us at the time of our repentance. He smiles over us when we begin the growth process with repentance, long before we attain maturity. Jesus feels compassion over the prodigals on the day they repent. The newly repentant yet immature prodigal son had many areas of his life that still needed transformation. God feels gladness and enjoyment for His prodigals on the day they repent. In the Biblical account of the "prodigal son," the prodigal's father made this known by giving his prodigal son the best robes and family ring on the very day he returned. The parable of the prodigal son is not primarily about a son who lost his inheritance, but about a father who lost his son and how the father gets his son back. We can have a new beginning with God as a first class citizen after we sincerely repent. We "push delete" after we have sincerely repented.

We relate to God by the means in which He has laid forth in His Word, on His terms, on the basis of who He is, who He says we are to Him and how we are to relate to Him. The Spirit of Jesus the Son lives in us. Through His Son we build relationship with our Father in Heaven. The same confident love, privilege, and assurance that Jesus enjoyed are now offered freely to us as sons and daughters. Jesus even goes as far to say that the love that the Father has for Him is the SAME love the Father has for you and I! (John 17:24,26)

Because of sin, lack of true repentance, and bad experiences and examples with natural fathers, it's not always easy to relate to God as our Father. Nevertheless, the Truth remains and beckons us to believe that God is our Father in Heaven. He's full of mercy, compassion, truth, power, affection and desire for our relationship with Him to be healthy and whole. We are called to be bold and confident sons and daughters who know who our Father is. The Father crushed the Son on the cross in order for this to be a reality offered to us. He's serious about us. He's serious about being our Father and us being His children.

Consider the "beholding and becoming" principle – whatever we behold (meditation unto revelation) in God's heart towards us becomes awakened in our heart back to God (transformation). 2 Cor. 3:18 talks about, "Beholding…the glory of the Lord…being transformed into the same image from glory to glory." Beholding God's heart refers to studying about it, speaking of it, and praying it until we understand and thus encounter truth and are changed/transformed on the inside. As we change our mind (understanding) about God then He changes our emotions and unlocks our hearts to love more. We are empowered to walk in righteousness more as we grow in our understanding of the love of God. Wrong understanding about God damages our hearts and causes disability in our walk. God wants to empower us to be lovers of God, thus He reveals Himself as a lover to us.

One emotion of our Father that is easy to grasp is His gladness. We will struggle comprehending His affection for us until we have a foundational understanding of His gladness. The Father's capacity for gladness is infinite in measure and eternal in duration. He designed the human spirit in His image, with great capacity for gladness. This is huge! What an invitation! As we become students of God's emotions, we grow in revelation of His tender mercy, His gladness, and His affection. With this understanding of our Father, when we stumble in sin, we will run to Him with confidence and sincere repentance instead of running from Him in condemnation and shame.

How does your Father feel when He looks at you? This question is one of the most important questions in our spiritual journey. Our view of God's emotions affects how we approach God, especially in our weakness and stumbling. When we get a glimpse of a God who possesses the fullness of joy in His presence (on His Throne, Revelation 4) we get confident in our joy. This becomes our strength (Neh 8:10) and our ability to be joyful in all circumstances. When stressful situations arise I close my eyes and picture my Father in Heaven and I'm settled and comforted when I see that gladness is in His place (1 Chron 16:27). Jesus was a master at this.

"I think of you"...what a powerful reality. This is what He's like; it's almost too good to be true. He governs all of creation and He thinks of me. When I'm going, when I'm coming, when I'm sleeping, when I'm traveling, when I'm at home, when I'm working... "I have thoughts of you," says God. Jeremiah 29:11 says, "For I know the thoughts that I think toward you, says the Lord, thoughts of peace and not of evil, to give you a future and a hope."

David had firsthand knowledge with the thoughts of God over him. In Psalm 139:17-18 he writes, "How precious also are Your thoughts to me, O God! How great is the sum of them! If I should count them, they would be more in number than the sand..." In Psalm 40:5 he writes, "Your thoughts toward us cannot be recounted to You in order; if I would declare and speak of them, they are more than can be numbered." First Samuel 13 is the first time that David is mentioned in scripture. God speaks of him to the prophet Samuel. God says that he is a "man after His own heart."

God had been thinking of David for some time. In 1 Samuel 16 the prophet Samuel goes to the house of Jesse to seek out this man (David turns out to be a teenage boy). My question has always been: what was David doing at the moment in time when God was whispering to Samuel about him back in chapter 13? It could've went something like this: David's doing his mundane, same-old, same-old duties and little did he know that the Father of Glory, the Ancient of Days who wraps Himself in light, was talking about him to the greatest prophet of the day. The God who has no bounds, holds the stars in His hands, tells the lightning where to strike and the seas where to stop... this is the God who is talking to Samuel about this shepherd boy who He's been watching and thinking about.

Here are some verses to ponder that reveal how much God delights in His sons and daughters. Ps 16:3 "As for the saints who are on the earth, 'They are the excellent ones, in whom is all my delight.'" Job 33:26 "He shall pray to God, and He will delight in him, he shall see His face with joy..." Prov 8:30 "And I was daily His delight, rejoicing always before Him..." Isa 62:4 "But you shall be called Hephzibah, and your land Beulah; for the Lord delights in you." Deut 30:9 "The Lord your God will make you abound in all the work of your hand...for the Lord will again rejoice over you for good as He rejoiced over your fathers..." Jeremiah 32:41 "Yes, I will rejoice over them to do them good, and I will assuredly plant them in this land, with all My heart and with all My soul." Zeph 3:17 "The Lord your God in your midst, the Mighty One, will save; He will rejoice over you with gladness, He will quiet you with His love, He will rejoice over you with singing."

We must apply our name to every verse above and say it back to God. When we hear the words and speak them with our mouths, it speeds the process of belief in our own hearts and has impact on our feelings and thoughts about God. The thoughts of the Father over you are inspired by His delight in you. His delight, pleasure, enjoyment, and joy are in you. We don't have to be "working" for the Kingdom to earn His delight. This is who God is. He loves us and this love awakens love/service to Him (1 John 4:19, John 3:16).

Chapter twelve

Beholding God

One of the things I learned during my time in leadership at IHOP-KC is the "beholding and becoming" principle: Whatever emotions we behold (by meditation) about God's heart towards us are imparted to our heart for God (transformation). Essentially, what we understand about God's heart transforms our emotions. When God wants to empower us to love Him, He reveals Himself as the One who loves us. We are dedicated to God, enjoy and pursue Him because we understand that He is dedicated to us, enjoys us, and pursues us. "We love Him because (we understand that) He first loved us." (1 John 4:19)

When we change our mind or understanding about God, then God changes our hearts or emotions. Wrong ideas about God's personality are what hinder our intimacy with Him. God wants us to have liberty. This means experiencing freedom in our emotions from condemnation, shame, fear, addiction, spiritual dullness or bondage. Wherever the Spirit is encountered there will be liberty.

The new covenant includes God writing His Word on our mind and heart. "This is the covenant (promise) that I will make with them…'I will put My laws (Word) into their hearts (emotions) and in their minds (understanding) I will write them…'" (Hebrews 10:16)

Here, God promises to empower our emotions until we actually desire righteousness. He also promises to release understanding to us so we can enjoy God and His Word.

The quality of our beholding the Lord is "dim" just like a mirror was in the ancient world. We all "gaze dimly" or lack clarity and focus in the process of coming before Him in prayer and meditation. This is the only type of beholding that God requires from us. "For now we see in a mirror, dimly, but then face to face." (1 Cor. 13:12) We come with confidence and boldness without any shame because Jesus paid the price. We come with the full assurance that God desires to help us draw near to His heart. "Having boldness to enter the Holiest by the blood of Jesus, by a new and living way...let us draw near with a true heart in full assurance of faith..." (Heb. 10:19-22)

Only the supernatural work of the Spirit can change the human heart. Thus, we must cooperate with the Spirit and cultivate a friendship with Him being careful not to quench or resist Him. The Spirit is our only escort into God's presence. We cannot go forward if the Spirit is quenched in our life. We must renounce anything that causes the Spirit's work in us to be minimized.

God's glory includes the revelation of His emotions. Exodus 33:18-19 tells of Moses' request before God: "Moses said, 'Please, show me Your glory.' He said, 'I will make My goodness pass before you, and I will proclaim the name of the Lord before you...'" Moses prayed to see God's glory or His beauty. God answered Moses by promising to reveal His name to him. In other words, to proclaim or make known His character or personality. Moses prayed with urgency, "Please, show me Your glory." He pleaded with God to talk to him about His glory or His personality. God has the best personality in the universe. He is the most passionate, kind, good, pure, happy, joyful, smart, mysterious, gentle, and bold Person in existence.

God revealed His glory to Moses by proclaiming His power and wisdom. However, the pinnacle of God's glory in this passage is when God revealed His emotions to Moses. "The Lord passed before him and proclaimed, 'The Lord, the Lord God, merciful and gracious, longsuffering and abounding in goodness and truth...'" (Exodus 34:6) We will be discussing some of these amazing attributes of God as we move along.

The Lord is merciful: He is tender in how He relates to us in our weaknesses and sin. This is the first aspect of His personality that He revealed to Moses because it is the one we need first.

1) The Lord delights in mercy. It is one of His favorite things to do in leading the universe. He enjoys the heart response of His people as we encounter His relentless mercy. "Who is...like You, pardoning iniquity...because He delights in mercy." (Mic. 7:18)

2) God's mercy is beyond anything we can compare to it. He gives it to all who repent. "Let the wicked forsake his way...let him return to the Lord, and He will have mercy on him...for He will abundantly

pardon. 'For My thoughts are not your thoughts, nor are your ways My ways,' says the Lord. 'For as the heavens are higher than the earth, so are My ways higher than your ways, and My thoughts than your thoughts.'" (Isa. 55:7-9)

3) God offers us a new start every day if we will only repent of our compromises. "Through the Lord's mercies we are not consumed, because His compassions fail not. They are new every morning; great is Your faithfulness." (Lam. 3:22-23)

4) David had great confidence in God's mercy or gentleness. "Your gentleness has made me great." (Ps. 18:35)

5) God wants us to have confidence before Him in love so that we run to God instead of from God when we encounter our sin and weakness. Knowing the Word and feeling some of God's affection for us gives us confidence and boldness even in our weakness.

The Lord is gracious: He is generous in how He relates to us in our labors. He rewards us or pays us so well for our efforts to obey and serve Him. He remembers every act of obedience. This dignifies and sanctifies every hour of our day. The smallest and seemingly insignificant acts of service and obedience are remembered and rewarded by God forever. "For God is not unjust to forget your work and labor of love which you have shown toward His name, in that you have ministered to the saints..." (Heb. 6:10)

1) The Lord is gracious in that He evaluates us differently than anyone else does. He remembers our frailty and that we are but dust (Ps. 103:14). The lifestyle that God calls us to live is within the reach of the weak (1 Jn. 5:4; Mt. 11:30). "He has not dealt with...nor punished us according to our iniquities." (Ps. 103:10)

2) He is neither like a harsh military leader nor an angry coach who rejects all weakness. "For He knows our frame; He remembers that we are dust." (Ps. 103:14)

3) God's presence is full of joy because God's heart or personality is full of joy. "In Your presence is fullness of joy; at Your right hand are pleasures..." (Ps 16:11)

4) Gladness and joy are at the center of Jesus' personality. The Holy Spirit imparts Jesus' joy to us through revealing the knowledge of God to us as we feed on God's Word.

5) Many people think of God as being mostly mad or mostly sad when He relates to us. The revelation of a God with a smiling heart awakens a smiling heart in us. This revelation releases security in us with a free spirit instead of being dominated by condemnation.

The Lord is longsuffering: He bears long with us instead of "writing us off." He does not lose enthusiasm for us when we fail. He does not retaliate in the way man does. "Do you despise the riches of His goodness, forbearance, and longsuffering, not knowing that the goodness of God leads you to repentance?" (Rom. 2:4)

1) He suffers long with our sinful responses. His love for us is greater than the pain we cause Him when we resist Him.

2) Understanding this gives us confidence that our repentance is never rejected.

The Lord is abounding in goodness: He overflows with good plans for us. The song that is recorded most often in Scripture is: "The Lord is good, His mercy endures forever." (1 Chr. 16:34, 41; 2 Chr. 5:13; 7:3, 6; 20:21; Ezra 3:11; Jer. 33:11; Ps. 100:5; 106:1; 107:1; 118:1; 138:8; 136) "I know the thoughts that I think toward you...thoughts of peace and not of evil, to give you a future and a hope. Then you will call upon Me...and I will listen to you." (Jer. 29:11-12) "No good thing will He withhold from those who walk uprightly." (Ps. 84:11)

Some resist God's mercy and goodness because it is so free that no one can ever deserve it. God's mercy is freely offered to us because Jesus fully satisfied the claims of God's justice by His death. Propitiation speaks of God's justice being appeased or satisfied by the offering of the blood of Jesus so that sinners can be freely accepted by God. Romans 3:24-26 states how, "Being justified freely by His grace through the redemption that is in Christ Jesus, whom God set forth as a propitiation by His blood...that He might be just and the justifier of the one who has faith in Jesus."

God shows us His mercy without violating His justice. He forgives sin because He paid for it. Jesus' propitiatory sacrifice on the cross does not cause God to love us. It removes the penalty that our sin deserves so we can experience His love in a way that is consistent with His justice. Jesus referred to Moses' experience in Exodus 33-34, when He promised to declare God's name or personality to us. God imparts love in us as we gain more understanding of what God is like. "I (Jesus) have declared to them Your name, and will declare it, that the love with which You loved Me may be in them..." (Jn. 17:26)

Paul's prayer for revelation in Ephesians 1:17 is similar to Moses' prayer to see God's glory in Exodus 33:18. "The Father of glory may give to you the spirit of wisdom and revelation in the knowledge of Him, the eyes of your understanding being enlightened..." (Eph. 1:17-18)

One of the great things we get to do as sons and daughters of God is to behold His glory—which is His emotions, power, and wisdom. We get to be involved in a real relationship where we get real exposure to the One in whom we belong. Real relationship means you let people in and you wear your heart on your sleeve...in other words real relationship means being vulnerable.

"For if what is passing away (old covenant) was glorious, what remains is much more glorious...Where the Spirit of the Lord is, there is liberty. But we all, with unveiled face, beholding as in a mirror the glory of the Lord, are being transformed into the same image (character) from glory to glory, just as by the Spirit of the Lord." (2 Cor. 3:11-18) In 2 Cor. 3, Paul compared the old and new covenants (v. 6-11). The old covenant was glorious because it provided forgiveness, yet it did not give the power to walk in righteousness. The new covenant is much more glorious because it allows us to behold, or encounter, the Lord in a way that gives us liberty and the power to be transformed in our hearts (v. 17-18). Beholding God's glory means to look at (study or encounter) His emotions, power, and wisdom as seen in creation, redemption, and His leadership over history.

The most effective way to begin to behold Gods Glory is by filling our minds with information about God's emotions from the Scripture. We can turn the Word into a dialog with God as we prayer-read it. Prayer, fasting, meditation on the Word, and obedience position our hearts before God to freely receive. These activities do not earn us God's favor or blessing in our lives. They do bring us into a deeper place of strength and maturity as a believer. When you learn to press past the friction of getting personal with God you will learn that when you get that breakthrough it pays off in your earthbound relationships. It is as if we put our cold heart before the bonfire of God's presence by seeking Him in the Word in spirit and truth.

Chapter thirteen

Cultivating Love

It is the inheritance of every believer to be transformed by encountering God's glory. The inheritance of every believer includes being exhilarated by feeling God's affection and pleasure for us and in feeling it back for Him. We were created to long to feel God's love. God created us to love Him in four spheres of our life, which include our heart (emotions), soul (identity), mind (thoughts) and strength (resources). He loves us in these same ways. These four distinct spheres of life do not automatically develop without our involvement. Mark 12:30 tells how, "You shall love the Lord your God with all your heart, with all your soul, with your entire mind, and with all your strength." Cultivating love for God is the first priority to God and the first emphasis of the Holy Spirit. "You shall love the Lord...this is the first and great commandment." (Matthew 22:37-38)

Cultivating love for God has the greatest impact on God's heart, our heart and on others. Cultivating love for God is the greatest calling. Some who seek to know God's will for their life focus on knowing what they are supposed to do instead of what they are supposed to become. When they speak of wanting the greatest calling, they refer to the size of their ministry instead of the size of their heart. The greatest grace we can receive is the anointing to feel God's love and to express it. It brings the greatest freedom and has the greatest reward in the age to come.

"The four main spheres of love are heart, mind, strength and soul."

Sphere #1) Love with all our heart: We love God with our emotions (affections), which are the very impulse of desire that affects our decisions. We have a significant role in determining how our emotions develop over time. We can "set" our love or affections on anything that we choose. Our emotions eventually follow whatever we set ourselves to pursue. As we change our mind, the Spirit changes our heart (emotions). "Because he has set his love (heart) upon Me, therefore I will deliver him..." (Ps. 91:14)

Sphere #2) Love with all our mind: We love God with our mind by taking the time and effort to come into agreement with the truth about Him and His purposes. This involves refusing lies about His ways and His heart. He is a tender Father and passionate Bridegroom King. We can fill our mind with that which inspires love for God instead of what diminishes it. Our mind is the doorway to our inner man that greatly affects our capacity to love. Much of our life occurs in our mind.

The language of the human spirit is images or pictures. Our mind is an internal movie screen that continually shows us pictures. It is like a camera that stores our memories. Our mind is a vast universe within us that will never be turned off. We cannot shut down the images in our mind, but we can direct them by meditating on God's Word. We can replace dark thoughts with new ones and thus we can rewrite the script of the movie that we continually watch within.

Sphere #3) Love with all our strength: This is to love God with our natural resources (time, money, energy, talents, words and influence). We express our love for God in the way we use our resources. The normal way to use them is to increase our personal comfort and honor. God sees us as we express our love to Him by investing our strengths into our relationship with God and His purposes. By doing this we sow our strengths into "God's bank." He multiplies and then returns our investment back to us. However, He does it in His own timing and way. "Your Father who sees in secret will reward you openly." (Mt. 6:18)

The principle of the fasted lifestyle is found in 2 Corinthians 12:9, "My grace is sufficient for you, for My strength is made perfect in weakness…" Fasting is to voluntarily embrace weakness so that God's strength is made perfect in us. We fast our strengths in the four ways in the Sermon on the Mount (Mt. 6:1-18). We serve and give (6:1-4, 19-21), pray (6:5-13), bless adversaries (forgive, 6:14-15; 5:44), and fast food (6:16-18). We embrace fasting or "voluntary weakness" in these four areas. We fast our time by praying, our money by giving, our words by blessing our enemies and our energy by fasting food. We fast by investing our natural strengths (time, money, energy, etc.) into the hands of the Spirit.

Sphere #4) Love with all our soul: We need to establish our identity in our relationship with God instead of in our accomplishments and in the recognition we receive from people. Our identity is determined by the way we define our success and value and thus, how we see ourselves. God's love for us is what truly determines our personal worth. We must define our success as being ones who are loved and chosen by God and who love God in return. We are to be anchored in this truth as the basis of our success and worth, rather than in our accomplishments, recognition, possessions or relationships. Our identity must be established on being loved by God and in loving Him instead of on our accomplishments or failures.

Our confession is, "I am loved (by God) and I am a lover (of God), therefore I am successful." Burnout does not come from working hard, but from working with a wrong spirit. When we work for success we get burned out. When we work from success our spirit is strengthened. As we change the way we define success, we will love God much better because we will have much less "emotional traffic" inside our heart and mind. We must refuse to live out of a false identity based on our accomplishments or failures. We are not to live a shame-based life, but one based in confidence in the grace of God.

Jesus is the premier example of loving God with all of His soul by living with a right identity. Jesus' identity is in love and humility. His humility was expressed when He became a man and died on the cross. In Philippians 2:6-8, we gain insight into how Jesus carried His heart before people: "Who being in the form of God, did not consider it robbery (something to be grasped, NIV) to be equal with God, but made Himself of no reputation (nothing NIV; emptied Himself NAS), taking the form of a bondservant, and coming in the likeness of men. And being found in appearance as a man, He humbled Himself and became obedient to the point of death..." Jesus did not consider it robbery to be equal to God in privilege and honor. There are two ways to apply this. First, Jesus would not have "taken" anything from God by insisting on enjoying the privileges that were rightfully His by virtue of being God. Secondly, He did not "take" anything from Himself by refusing the privileges of being treated as equal to God.

After the incarnation, Jesus had two natures, being fully God and fully man. He was never less than God, but He lived on earth as though He was never more than a man. Being in the form of God, He had the power to influence people. He only used it when He was led by the Spirit. He lived as every other godly person by praying, obeying and waiting on the Spirit's leadership. Jesus emptied Himself of the right to take the initiative to use the fullness of God's power.

Jesus emptied Himself of His reputation in the eyes of man. He embraced a lifestyle where everyone underestimated Him and His abilities. People never knew how superior His abilities were. When they saw Him, they saw nothing to distinguish Him. He was happy to be seen as an ordinary man without any special form (status) or comeliness (attractiveness). "He has no form or comeliness; and when we see Him, there is no beauty that we should desire Him. He is despised and rejected by men...and we did not esteem Him." (Isa. 53:2-3)

What was most important to Him was to tell the Father's story and to change forever the lives of people by dying for them. If His core identity was in having power, then His incarnation would have been a denial of His true self. For all eternity, He delights in humility. It was not something He was only while on earth. It is something that He is. His humility did not begin at the incarnation. Jesus did not serve to prove something, but to express the truth about Himself. It is precisely because Jesus is God that He served and gave freely to ungrateful men (Lk. 6:35). There was nothing un-Godlike about washing the disciples' feet. He was at home doing this. We are to love God with all our soul by stewarding His calling and blessing on our life with a servant identity, instead of in our influence and abilities or in how big our business or ministry is.

We love God by loving and honoring the people He called and who are dear to Him. We must not regard men after the flesh by seeing them based on what they accomplish (2 Cor. 5:16). We are to see them as God sees them, recognizing His heart for them and His plan to use them. The Holy Spirit is the guardian of the culture of the Body of Christ. He requires that we dwell together in a culture of honor. God's love is experienced most as we honor each other. Part of our inheritance and what we lack is in the hands of others. We can receive this by blessing them. Blessing is not the same as unconditional tolerance of everyone's doctrines and practices.

Receiving revelation of God's heart for specific people (ministries) convinces us that God greatly desires to bless them. This makes it easy for us to bless them. Blessing comes from honor. We must demonstrate a culture of honor in our personal families and in our ministry assignment (church, marketplace, school, neighborhood, etc.). "In honor giving preference to one another...Bless and do not curse. Rejoice with those who rejoice...Do not be wise in your own opinion..." (Rom. 12:10-18) We can bless people's budding virtues that have not yet matured, regardless of their deficiencies in ministry. We can do this without needing to agree with or endorse their differences in ministry focus, style, and standards of excellence. The Spirit forbids us to verbalize such deficiencies and differences. We should speak affirmations that we believe, without any flattery. As for rejoicing, we need to be able to celebrate the increase others receive. We should not presume to understand all that God sees in those around us.

Understanding God's kindness, His value of His people and His desire to use all His people convinces us of their value to the Kingdom and our need of them. However, the natural bias of the human heart is elitism that seeks to be best and speaks without a spirit of inclusion. Ask the Lord to show you how He sees others. After we see their value and virtues, then we feel differently about their deficiencies. God is ravished for each of His people and has an agenda for each that is important to Him. The miracle of mercy is that God uses us, even in our weakness and sin. The reason we have future usefulness in His Kingdom is because God is kind to evil men (Luke 6:35). The same confidence we have that God will use us on the basis of kindness is the confidence we have in God using others.

Chapter fourteen

Getting Back to the First Commandment

God called Israel to hear His heart throughout the scriptures both Old and New. Jesus' most repeated exhortation in the New Testament was, "He that has an ear, let him hear" (Mt. 11:15; 13:9, 43; Mk. 4:9, 23; 7:16; Lk. 8:8; 14:35; Rev. 2:7, 11, 17, 29; 3:6, 13, 22; 13:9). "Hear (Shema), O Israel: The Lord our God, the Lord is one! You shall love the Lord your God with all your heart, with all your soul, and with all your strength." (Deut. 6:4-5) Jesus interpreted what they were meant to "hear." Namely, that loving God is His first priority and what He considers the greatest way to live. We must press to the limits of what the words "first" and "great" imply.

Do not apologize for your intensity in your vision to love Jesus. "You shall love the Lord...This is the first and great commandment." (Mt. 22:37-38) The Shema reveals the "why" behind the "what" of creation and redemption. God's ultimate purpose for creation is to provide a family for Himself and an eternal companion for Jesus who would be equally yoked to Him in love. Jesus' inheritance is a people He fully possesses in love. "I (the Father) will give You (Jesus) the nations for Your inheritance..." (Ps. 2:8) God will cause all creation to obey Jesus (Phil. 2:9-11). God will also raise up a people equally yoked in love. He wants us to love Him with all of our heart and mind because He loves us with all of His heart and mind.

As a King, Jesus will be obeyed, but as a Bridegroom, He will be loved. A king's inheritance is to rule over obedient subjects. A bridegroom's inheritance is partnership with a loving bride. We must continually realign our life and ministry to make the First Commandment our first priority. By the very definition of love, we must invite Him. He will not force us into a relationship of voluntary love. He waits until we invite Him in the matters of our heart. God's purpose is to select and train a Bride who would be prepared by voluntary love to reign with Jesus.

The First Commandment will be in first place in the Church when Jesus returns. "For the marriage of the Lamb has come, and His wife has made herself ready." (Rev. 19:7) He will supernaturally empower us to love Him this way. It takes "God to love God." "The love of God has been poured out in our hearts by the Holy Spirit..." (Rom. 5:5) Jesus prayed for His people to be supernaturally empowered to love Him with God's love. "I declared...Your name...that the love with which You loved Me may be in them." (Jn. 17:26)

Loving God is the first priority to God. Jesus did not call it the first option, but a commandment. This is the first emphasis of the Holy Spirit. Loving God is a glorious end in itself. However, it never ends with loving God, but always overflows into loving ourselves and others. The Song of Solomon has two main sections. Song 1-4 is focused on the Bride receiving her inheritance in Jesus. Song 5-8 is focused on Jesus receiving His inheritance in the Bride. Since loving God is His first priority, we must plan our ministries with this as our first goal and measurement of success. Numerical growth is good, but that is not the litmus test of God's favor. I ask the Spirit to mark all of us so that this is our top priority in our ministry mission statement.

God has everything, yet He is searching for something. What does God search for? What does He want most and first? It is love that He is after. He is after our heart. He wants our voluntary love. When we find what God is looking for, then we will find the answer to what we are looking for. "True worshipers will worship the Father in spirit and truth; for the Father is seeking such to worship Him...Those who worship Him must worship in spirit and truth." (Jn. 4:23-24)

I love worshiping God and I don't think there are many things that can compare with singing to my Father; however there is a revelation I have now that I didn't have before. When I say of worshiping in spirit and truth I am talking about worshiping from an authentic heart where you are open before the Lord hiding nothing from Him. When you align yourself with the truth of who God is and the truth of who you are in Him then you worship from a deeper place that is filled with authenticity and power.

Many are searching to know God's will. The first issue in God's will is to love Him. The mystery of our life is found in this truth. He wants us. We cry, "Lord, what are You doing in my life? Why are You allowing certain things?" He is after our heart. God does everything for love. Christianity is an ongoing encounter of love with a

Person. A deep sense of mission to change a city or nation will not keep us steady unless we encounter Jesus in love. The labor of ministry makes us weary without the consistent stirring of love in our emotions by the Spirit.

Loving God is the greatest thing we can do. It has the greatest impact on God's heart and ours. Our greatest calling is to move God's heart and to be moved by God's heart. We touch Him by every movement of our heart to show love to Him by obedience. It is the most extreme lifestyle. Do you know the way that you move Him? Each time we repent of compromise it moves Him. We move His heart by sitting before Him (Lk. 10:38-42) and by doing small acts of service for others because of love for Him (Heb. 6:10; Mt. 10:42). Our greatest satisfaction is to know and feel His love, to love Him and to overflow in love for others. Our identity is found in this. I confess, "I'm loved (by God) and I am a lover (of God), therefore I am successful." This is what we look like to God. Loving Jesus has the greatest reward in the age-to-come and thus, it is the only way to enter our greatest destiny. You can be one of the greatest people in history by loving God (Mt. 5:19).

Jesus defined loving God as being deeply rooted in a spirit of obedience (Jn. 14:21; Deut. 6:1-9). There is no such thing as loving God without seeking to obey His Word. Loving God requires more than singing to Him or having sentimental feelings about a "god we make in our image." "If you love Me, keep My commandments...He who has My commandments and keeps them, it is he who loves Me...If anyone loves Me, he will keep My word..." (Jn. 14:15-23) What does Jesus command us to do? He commands us to love Him, ask Him for things, be near Him, and enjoy His glory with His liberating holiness. His commands are related to loving Him. "This is the love of God, that we keep His commandments. His commandments are not burdensome." (1 Jn. 5:3)

There are three types of obedience: affection-based, duty-based, and fear-based. "Affection-based obedience" is obedience that flows from experiencing Jesus' affection for us and giving it back to Him. It is the strongest, deepest and most consistent obedience. Why? Because a lovesick person will endure anything for love. "Duty-based obedience" is our commitment to obedience even if we do not feel God's presence. God's Word requires that we obey God without feeling inspired to do so. "Fear-based obedience" is obedience motivated by the fear of negative consequences. It is biblical to appeal to shame and fear to motivate people. Scripture has many "do's and don'ts" such as do not commit adultery, steal, etc. We sin when our heart is unsatisfied with God.

Obedience based on affection does not need the pressure of added difficulty (God's discipline), shame (being caught), or to be watched to avoid dishonesty with money, laziness, porn, etc. Our greatest strengthening is found in affection-based obedience that flows from experiencing Jesus' affection and responding back in love. It is the most consistent obedience because a lovesick person will endure anything for love. People in love are untouchable. We can set our hearts to live as extravagant lovers of God without getting trapped into bitterness toward those who mistreat us. What is your greatest dream for your life? The anointing to love God is our greatest possession. The reward of love is found in possessing the power to love. No sacrifice is comparable to what He gives us in His love. Anyone can quit, but a person in love.

We need revelation of the supremacy of the First Commandment. It is the standard of evaluation at the Judgment Seat of Christ. God measures life differently than men because He has all the money, wisdom, fame, influence and time. What will matter is whether we grew in love for God. We are not left guessing as to what God considers greatest. In seeking to stay up with popular ministry trends, some regularly change directions in their ministry. We must not get our ministry focus from the latest trend, but from God's Word. God is raising up forerunner messengers to call others to define love as God's highest purpose. They will make the First Commandment their primary focus for their life and ministry.

The Church of Ephesus was a great revival center in the early Church (Acts 19-20), yet, they did not sustain the freshness of their love for Jesus. They became workers for God more than lovers of God. Lovers will always outwork the workers. "I have this against you, that you have left your first love..." (Rev. 2:4) When we work without intimacy, we work as a slave or a hireling. Service without the foundation of devotion leads to burnout, disappointment, and wounding. Thus, the service is not sustained over decades. Our first loyalty and preoccupation is to Jesus, then secondly to His mission and our role in it. It is common to be preoccupied with the mission because it is deeply tied to our role and identity.

The power of martyrdom is found in being preoccupied with the First Commandment. The Book of Revelation is Jesus' plan to fill the earth with the First Commandment. "I saw…those who have the victory over the beast…standing on the sea of glass." (Rev. 15:2) "They overcame him (Satan) by the blood of the Lamb and by the word of their testimony, and they did not love their lives to the death." (Rev. 12:11)

We must make a determined decision to set our heart to make loving God our first priority. We must establish a vision to go deep in God. This will require much focus and continual effort. It also requires that we must be focused on pursuing it more than gaining things and influence. "Because he has set his love upon Me, therefore I will deliver him…" (Ps. 91:14) The power of articulating your love and gratitude to Jesus is often overlooked. It will change your life to regularly say out loud, "Jesus, I love You. I thank and trust You."

To receive love from the Father is to give love in wisdom and power to those around us…with love comes identity and destiny…

Chapter fifteen

Restoration, the love language of God

I was talking with a friend of mine who is a pastor in another state and he was having an issue with a worship leader at his church. Instead of working things out with the worship leader and getting him healing, they decided to remove him so they would not be associated with his issues. I don't recall Jesus doing this with the disciples or us. Jesus was desperately committed to restoration, even unto death. After the phone conversation with my pastor friend, a few weeks went by. I thought I would give him a call. When I called they had made it official and removed the worship leader.

All of a sudden, I got this idea and thought to myself this is interesting. So, I told him we were having the same issue at the church I was helping lead and he said, "Oh?" I began to expound on a worship leader we had who was very famous. I said this worship leader was known all over the world and we just hired him, but we had a problem. My friend asked me what the issue was. I told him that this worship leader was in a very dark place. I said he had an affair with a married woman. My friend said, "Oh man, get him out of there before your reputation suffers."

I said, "It gets worse...this worship leader actually fell in love with this married woman and she got pregnant." This sent my friend through the roof and he was adamant about publically expelling this worship leader. I told my friend one more time, "It gets much worse." He asked, "How could it get any worse?" I began to tell him, "Man, this worship leader tried to cover his own tracks and we just found out he had the husband of the woman killed." My friend said, "That worship leader will never be in ministry ever again!" My friend then asked me for the name of this worship leader so he could make people he knew aware. I told him, "His name is King David." My pastor friend was beside himself. He simply could not believe what had just taken place. He was silent for a moment on the phone and then said, "I understand. Thank you."

So what is restoration after all? Do any of us really know? The answer is yes we can look up the definition and that should give you a good context. The definition from Dictionary.com reads like this: Restoration is "A return of something to a former, original, normal, or unimpaired condition" or "Something that is restored, as by renovating. "

Definition: the act of restoring

Synonyms: alteration, cure, healing, rebuilding, reclamation, recovery, reestablishment, reformation, rehabilitation, rejuvenation, remaking, remodeling, renewal, renovation, return, revival

You can see just by simply reading the definition that restoration is a really amazing thing. That someone who has fallen from there royal position in the Kingdom can be put back into that position as well as experiencing greater glory through that re-establishment. When you read through the synonyms concerning restoration it brings a level of understanding that otherwise would be lost. Revival is one of the synonyms for restoration, so not only are you put back into your position but you also do so in revival. When you think about being re-established to your former glory in the very spirit of revival it means for us a restoration to life, consciousness, vigor, strength, etc. So not only do you get to get back into your position, but you also get strength & consciousness which means sobriety and levity, and levity is defined as character.

So what is the fruit of restoration? Well If someone is restored to a leadership position and is racked with insecurities about their position then that is the fruit that the reconciliation to their former position was not done correctly either by the one restoring or the one who is restored. What I mean is that if there is an unhealthy amount of self-persecution and shame in the individual being restored there heart didn't connect with the true process and ultimate the true reason for their restoration. Conviction, grief, guilt, and being repentant are only appropriate before you ask for forgiveness not after you have been forgiven and restored. When you are forgiven for a sin it is no longer necessary to keep repenting for that same sin. You must walk in confidence in the strength of the Lord and His ability to truly forgive.
When you are working with people who need restoration due to sexual issues that is when things can become particularly difficult simply do to the complex nature of sexual brokenness. Often times when we as

church leaders are restoring someone it is due to the reason of immorality. That is the number one catalyst that the enemy uses to knock us out of or position of authority.

Many men in the bible have fallen for this very reason. In the life of David this is an overarching theme. David's first year as king of Israel he committed adultery with Bathsheba and Pre-Meditated Murder. The name Solomon comes from the root שלם(shalem 2401) meaning to be complete, sound. Derivative שלום(shalom 2401a) means peace. So the full meaning of the name Solomon is "Complete Peace." Although Psalm 91 is anonymous and tradition demands that Solomon is the great peace-king, his name may have stemmed from David's deep remorse and grief over losing Solomon's older sibling.

Often times people bring our ministry in to assist with church splits or moral failures and the one predominant question is "Is there one perfect way to restore someone?" and the answer is YES...the perfect model for restoration is to take each individual being restored as a unique person with unique issues. We get into trouble when we try to make everyone else fit into a mold of restoration. Something's work for some and those same things don't work for others who need restoration. Restoration is a customizing process if that makes sense.

In the process of restoration we should never put shame on an individual now guilt however can lead to repentance. Guilt is a public emotion that causes us to confess our sins to God and men, but shame is a private emotion that causes us to become more hidden and broken. All I know the process of restoration because when I was a young man I walked through restoration and now looking back I see the huge flaws as well as things that were good. Even though it was completely messy and a lot of really bad mistakes were made in the process of being restored the Lord was still able to work it for my good. I learned what not to do when restoring someone else which has been proven as a priceless tool to me all these years later. We work with restoring individuals, relationships, and churches now as a division of our ministry. Now in some cases when you have someone in your community who is continually doing harm those types of boundaries are an absolute necessity. Again the process of restoration is one that must be conducted by God through the wisdom of the Word and the leading of the Holy Spirit. It cannot be a process left to man alone or you will break someone's spirit…

Galatians 6:1-3 (ESV Version)

Bear One Another's Burdens
[1] Brothers, if anyone is caught in any transgression, you who are spiritual should restore him in a spirit of gentleness. Keep watch on yourself, lest you too be tempted. [2] Bear one another's burdens, and so fulfill the law of Christ. [3] For if anyone thinks he is something, when he is nothing, he deceives himself.

Galatians 6:1-3 has been a verse that many have used as a weapon to put shame on an individual who is going through restoration. I have been in leadership meetings and heard well-meaning pastors make statements like this "be careful restoring that brother, because if you're not careful you could fall into the same sin he is caught up in". However if you simply read this section of scripture and understand the nature and character of God you will see what the Lord is really saying through these verses. It doesn't have to do with falling into the same sin it is in reference to restoring someone in a spirit of gentleness, and not falling into judgment over the individual being restored. Restoration was never meant to be a simple and clean process. Just look at the crucifixion of Jesus Christ. There was nothing simple or clean about the process of crucifixion. I don't want to imply that there is a perfect way to restore someone and I have the revelation that others don't (quite the opposite actually) The truth is that people get hurt in the restoration process because we are dealing with wounds that are already there in the first place. It is a fearful and wonderful opportunity to get to assist someone in being restored to the Lord as well as restoration to community.

Some people have very strict demands that are appropriate for the measure of darkness they have come into agreement with while others have less strict boundaries due to the level of offense. We must use wisdom when walking saints through this sensitive process. Some people will not come out of there wound and deception without being shaken loose while others deception is not as deeply rooted and thus the time of getting to wholeness is greatly reduced.

Restoration must take place with several individuals and not just two people. The reason is due to the fact that the one restoring someone else must be accountable to others that are wise and mature in such areas. It doesn't work to have an immature believer navigate the complex process of restoration. It is always better to have a few people in on the process, now that doesn't mean that everyone needs to know the depths of what has landed an individual in restoration, but those brought in on the process must keep an eye on the situation making sure no level of abuse is going on. This is for the best interest of the individual as well.

Well I believe if you have control over the process of your restoration than that is the beginning signs that you are not really in the restoration process. When someone has fallen and they submit to restoration they are saying "I trust you Jesus with what I have done, and I trust who you have given charge over me". If you are being restored you don't get to enter into contractual negotiations in the sense of you can restore me but here are my concessions. However that being said you also do not want to submit to a system that is unhealthy, cultish, or violates your free will. God will never violate your free will and neither should the process of restoration. If you have submitted to restoration then you are doing so of your own free will. I believe that this is the major reason restorations don't go as planned. I think the individual who is submitting to restoration often times does so with deception in there heart and thereby entering in without free will but rather fear or a distorted perspective of what will take place in the process. That fear or wrong perspective could be due to a varied number of reasons, such as fear of separation, rejection, or isolation.

The entry point into accepting and acknowledging the need for restoration is based on trusting others with what you've done. The reason it is so important to be a person who is trustworthy to walk someone through the process of restoration is because you will be trusted on a large scale concerning what is good and healthy for an individual other than yourself. The whole point of entering into restoration and submitting to people is due to the fact that you are admitting you are deceived in a certain area and it has caused you to stumble into an unhealthy lifestyle or has brought an injustice to your family.

Restoration is not about a legalistic list of do's and don'ts. If there are no boundaries however then there is no process of restoration. Restoration is not about punishment, but rather it's about getting someone through a poor behavior that is based on personal deception. The way to assist with someone overcoming their poor behavior is through asserting Godly boundaries. The cure for poor behavior related to deception is Godly boundaries.

Sometimes when someone is going through the process of restoration they can often feel like boundaries are legalism and we must remember to discuss this aspect of restoration with the individual being restored. We don't want to feel like we need to control sin in others but rather we need to as leaders ask the Holy Spirit for help concerning where the boundaries need to be implemented. Each person is unique and that is why there is a great need for those who are restoring them to do so only under the power of the Holy Spirit.

It is common that Church leaders do not want to deal with restoring others because it can be very messy, demanding, and at times traumatic. I have met with many pastors who would rather turn a blind eye to the issues in there Church rather than confront the issues that oppose the Kingdom being built in their community. Restoration is not just about an individual being restored but it is also about the Kingdom being established in your community or church.

Restoration was the purpose of the Cross…it was to restore us back to God. We all fall short and are in desperate need of a savior…
There are many factors as to why restoration is important to God. In fact I believe one could write an entire book on just that subject. To address some of the factors would be beneficial for everyone involved in the process of restoration. Sometimes we need to be reminded why we need restoration, and because of deception we must be clear in our communication of this fact. Often times people struggle with admitting they even need restoration, due to their wound and deception they believe they can keep going in a lifestyle of sin or perhaps they believe it's not that bad in the first place.

Final Thoughts

My whole purpose in writing this book was to discuss what love looks like and by doing so we can know when we are not choosing love, because we now know love. I have such a strong desire for you the reader to go out there and love with your heart on your sleeve totally abandoned to the Heart of the Father. I want to see a people possessed by love and turning a city, a country, and a world over to the power of love and as we have established...God is love, so love rightly in truth with wisdom and revelation.

For more information on Luke Holter or Prophetic Sheep Ministries please feel free to visit their website at www.lukeholter.com

Please check out Luke's first book with Destiny Image Publishing titled "A Beautiful Kind of Broken"